# Faculty Development

## in a Time of Retrenchment

The Group for Human Development
in Higher Education

# The Group for Human Development in Higher Education

Alexander W. Astin
University of California
    at Los Angeles

Craig Comstock
The Wright Institute
Berkeley, California

David C. Epperson
Northwestern University
Evanston, Illinois

Andrew M. Greeley
National Opinion
    Research Center
University of Chicago

Joseph Katz
The Wright Institute (and)
State University of New York
    at Stony Brook

Joseph F. Kauffman
University of Wisconsin
Madison, Wisconsin

This report is being published under a grant from the Hazen Founda-
tion. The Carnegie Corporation, the Danforth Foundation, and the
Lilly Endowment helped underwrite the work of the Group for Human
Development in Higher Education.

# Preface

The members of the Group for Human Development in Higher Education are diverse in training, affiliations, and styles of teaching, research, and administration. They share a concern for improving the effectiveness of colleges and universities in furthering the development of all their members, whether students, faculty, or administrators. Three members of the group had earlier served on the Hazen Foundation committee that issued, in 1968, a report called *The Student in Higher Education*. With support from the Danforth Foundation the group has met repeatedly to explore the situation of faculty members, especially with regard to the quality of teaching.

Out of the range and intensity of these discussions came a shared approach to faculty development and a variety of major themes and proposals. Craig Comstock was asked to draw together the substance of these meetings, develop additional lines of thought, frame a set of recommendations, and draft this report on behalf of the group.

The grant from the Danforth Foundation supported the writing of the first version of the report, which, with the help of funds from the Carnegie Corporation and the Lilly Endowment, Inc., was considerably expanded. A grant from the Hazen Foundation has allowed *Change* to publish the report. We are grateful for the support the group has received, which of course implies no endorsement by the various grantors of what is said in this report.

The group also wants to thank Timothy Healy, who contributed to its early discussions of faculty development. Readers of one or another version of the report have included George Bonham, Laura Bornholdt, William L. Bradley, Margaret Comstock, Donald W. Light, Jr., Ernest A. Lynton, Mary Lowenthal Felstiner, Celia Morris, John Nason, David Riesman, Yosal Rogat, and Nevitt Sanford. We are grateful for their criticisms and suggestions. A special word of thanks is due the editors of *Change* for their help as publishers of the report.

Alexander W. Astin
Craig Comstock
David C. Epperson
Andrew M. Greeley
Joseph Katz
Joseph F. Kauffman

# About This Special Report

THERE IS A CURIOUS THING ABOUT TEACHING: IT IS AT ONCE the most central business in the college world, and yet it is the least talked about. Grumbled about, yes. But one rarely hears an intelligent discussion of it. Most faculty, I suspect, would rather keep things that way. One attends various academic conferences, and people act as if teaching were not their prime occupation. Or one sits at an editor's desk, as I do at *Change*, and one stares over a foot-high pile of manuscripts on higher learning and in it there is not a single intelligent tome on *how* one teaches.

All of this wouldn't strike me as odd if I didn't know that a lot of good teaching goes on, and that many faculty care deeply for successfully imparting their knowledge to their students. But these people are the exceptions now, and their talent seems not to be contagious. The demystification of higher learning continues, but here, in the inner core, in the art and technique of teaching, the veils remain in place.

And the revelation that now begins, I'm sorry to say, comes from other and often alien quarters: from disaffected students, from parents, disgruntled legislators, efficiency experts, and the remaining few who consider all teaching as an oppression of liberated adolescent consciousness, raised to the nth power.

There are a lot of nonsensical ideas going around about education these days, but I cannot include this dissatisfaction with college and university teaching as one of them. Efficiency cultists and budget-conscious legislatures may have their emphasis misplaced, but their complaints of large-scale ineffectiveness in the classroom are real and often justified. And many sensitive students become frustrated in their efforts to find teachers who know how to teach. It is one of the grosser tragedies of the present era in higher education that just as it has an historic opportunity to attract to the muse of higher learning large numbers of academically less talented students, our general abilities to imbue them with some larger intellectual sensitivities seem to have failed. As a consequence, much of what passes for higher education tends to dull the enthusiasms of thousands of new learners rather than strike fresh sparks of intellectual inquiry and curiosity.

During a recent visit to a liberal arts college, I asked a gifted and talented department chairman what his college specialized in. "We specialize in boredom," he said, and he was only half joking. It is a sad comment on lost human opportunities.

One knows, of course, that it can be otherwise. Wondrous and magical things do happen in college classrooms across the country, and some cynics might say that such superb teaching may well be wasted on the young. I doubt that it ever can be, although one wishes that exciting teaching were the rule rather than the exception.

To help accelerate the movement toward broader teaching excellence, Change Magazine publishes this important position paper on faculty development. The talents of the Group for Human Development in Higher Education, in an earlier and slightly different membership, became nationally recognized for a paper on student life, which was published by the Hazen Foundation several years ago. Their publication on the American college student quickly became a collector's item because of its unusual sensitivity to human values and the modesty of its presumptions. Both qualities occur rather rarely in academic communications.

This present effort is the result of a fortuitous collaboration between the Group for Human Development in Higher Education, as the authors of this report, the Hazen Foundation as the funding agency, and Change Magazine as the publisher. While publishers should perhaps not editorialize about their own works, the editors of Change decided to undertake this publication for several important and timely reasons. The present malaise on many of our campuses must soon be overcome if serious and essential efforts at internal improvement and performance are to take place. Making do with less can be a perfectly acceptable way of life, but goals must be clearly established at the outset. They must be set high so that the spirit of professional improvement is not constricted along with the budget.

We at *Change* attach particular importance to the idea that people in tight corners may find themselves more inventive than they would be in a less strained condition. The trends in higher education can now go two ways: either toward further disintegration, conservatism, and minimal risk taking; or to a new flowering of self-sufficiency, pride in the excellence of one's work, and a recognition that this new social role of the teacher can bring forth fresh energies and enthusiasms.

The recommendations in this paper are practical and within reach. They await no federal legislation or a signal from heaven. The report is modest in its inspiration and vision, but it ought not to be overlooked for this modesty, which is more deceptive than real. Were most of what it recommends put into practice on the majority of our campuses, we would have an educational revolution on our hands that would make the innovations of the last two decades look insignificant.

The best use of this position paper will undoubtedly vary from campus to campus. One cannot help but feel that one or two dozen copies, strategically distributed to the men and women who ordinarily make things happen on campus, might help develop change strategies that may surprise even veteran cynics. The glacial speed with which academic change traditionally comes about may be substantially accelerated by the presence of logical and modest concrete proposals, with which this volume abounds.

Thousands of thoughtful people in academic institutions will join us at *Change* in expressing gratitude to both the Group for Human Development in Higher Education and the Hazen Foundation for making this position paper possible. We shall follow its use and repercussions with particular interest.

George W. Bonham
March 1974

# The Professional Development of Faculty: Why, When, and How?

## 1
### The Need for Faculty Development
Professional stagnation among American faculty is in danger of replacing faculty mobility. Wringing more out of declining resources makes adequate teaching supports on a major scale all the more essential to assure faculty development through the end of this century. Page 13.

## 2
### Kinds of Reform
Why some old devices to encourage good teaching don't work, and what strategies may be used to achieve substantial improvements in the quality of college teaching. Some practical and reasonable departures from current practice can substantially enhance the professionalization of teaching. Page 19.

## 3
### Teaching as a Performing Art
Teaching, unlike research and publishing, remains very much a private professional act, rarely open to collegial scrutiny. Effective teaching remains a stepchild in the hierarchy of academic goals and values. It could be greatly improved by opening up the process to sensible and substantive criticism. Page 27.

## 4
### Knowledge About Learning
Self-reflectiveness about the processes of teaching and learning can become a viable instrument for teacher and student alike. Such awareness is rarely present today. An institutionalized intellectual concern for the nature of learning may represent the last remaining bit of common culture in the modern, diffused multiversity. Page 33.

## 5
### Training Future Professors
Few graduate schools prepare their students for teaching in any practical sense, leaving classroom performance largely to chance. A new teaching practicum, new teaching degrees, and the encouragement of intellectual work directed toward the classroom are some devices to upgrade current teaching effectiveness. Page 37.

## 6
### Campus Programs on Teaching
Most campuses suffer from an anemic pedagogical culture. New institutionwide programs for teaching would counteract the present undernourishment. Campus teaching institutes may be one remedy. If they are carefully planned, such teaching centers can produce a number of benefits of long-range significance both to participants and institutions. Page 45.

# 7
## The Role of Experts

Pedagogic development through teaching institutes may be further enhanced by teaching consultants from the outside, used in a suitable mix with the campus faculty. Expertise in this area should be utilized wherever it is available. Page 53.

# 8
## Evaluation for What?

The great game of grading offers relief from the ambiguities of learning, but the two should not be confused. Good learning presumes a vulnerability, which grading as a sorting-out process often prevents. A separation of the two is possible, with third-party assessment of both students and teachers performed in an atmosphere of confidentiality. Page 57.

# 9
## Grants for Teaching

National resources for enhancing pedagogical competence are woefully lacking, and grants should be provided similar to those given for research. The dual hierarchy of quality teaching and intellectual work and research needs to be legitimated, with grant dollars attached to both. Page 63.

# 10
## Intellectual Mobility

It is harder to improve an existing job than to move to a new one, but diminished faculty mobility may provide opportunities for in-place enhancing of professional competence. Multiple professional identifications, rather than identification only with one's own discipline, is a break with academic traditions that would provide networks of interests and intellectual integration. Page 67.

# 11
## Mid-Career Transitions

Providing insurance mechanisms to allow mid-career transitions into nonacademic work could make a very large difference to academic institutions in the late twentieth century. Intercampus faculty exchanges and provisions for mixing academic with nonacademic employment would also enhance academic performance in a period of contraction. Page 75.

# 12
## Ways to Begin

Seven key recommendations, and a discussion of how they would work. Strategies on how to begin revitalizing campus teaching, their hazards and their pay-offs. If the sixties was the decade of growth, the seventies and eighties can well become the decades of resourcefulness. Page 81.

# 1

# The
# Need
# for
# Faculty
# Development

Professional stagnation among American faculty is in danger of replacing faculty mobility. Wringing more out of declining resources makes adequate teaching supports on a major scale all the more essential to assure faculty development through the end of this century.

CRITICS OF HIGHER EDUCATION SOMETIMES LET SLIP THE urgency of their wish that professors would become, in their teaching, more sensitive, resourceful, deft, and responsive. Having thus implicitly complained, the critics often fail to specify how teachers can develop these undoubtedly useful qualities.

Some critics appear to believe that teaching would improve if only professors drawn astray by the sirens of research, or lulled by the boredom of pedagogical routine, had their classroom performances sharply evaluated. Other critics seem to hope that a new curriculum, style of teaching, form of governance, or more relevant purpose would generate the necessary qualities, as if a new system requiring sensitivity and endurance would necessarily also elicit them.

These viewpoints suggest a widespread academic reluctance to regard teaching in the same way the profession regards almost every other set of skills—as something that can be taught. In their roles as chemists, literary critics, or psychologists, professors often show painstaking care for method; but with regard to teaching, the academic culture is remarkably unreflective. In part this reluctance derives from the dreary record of many educationists who do profess to train teachers; in part, from the tendency of every profession to cloak its own processes in mystery as a way to achieve status; and in part, from the notion that an academic is valuable for what he knows, rather than for what he can help other people learn. As a result, professors may describe teaching as so straightforward that it requires no special training, and yet as so complex and idiosyncratic that mere training could never meet its extraordinary demands.

Helping professors to teach more effectively may, as some would argue, be unnecessary, impossible, or both; but the first view is not wholly sustained by the response of students and the second appears to violate a premise of the academic profession itself. Besides, the issue is not only training; the practice of any art generally benefits from colleagueship, knowledge about the effects of the art, rewards for good work, support for special projects, arrangements for collaboration, a knowledgeable audience, and so forth.

It is true that faculty can develop as teachers with hardly any of this, in settings nearly barren of responsiveness or support. There are teachers who do a good job despite a formidable set of handicaps. They have never been trained, except perhaps by assisting in a course while coping with the more urgent demands of graduate school. They have received little or no useful response to their work in the classroom. They have had to report on their own students for the benefit of third parties. They have had their teaching undervalued or crudely assessed by promotion and salary committees. They have been thwarted by tacit strictures on what, how, and with whom courses can be taught. And they have suffered the lack of a shared, disciplined current of knowledge among college teachers about how students learn.

Although many professors may achieve creditable results in spite of these and other disadvantages, a system of supports for teaching could lead to achievements more satisfying to professors and students alike. We shall subsequently set forth the elements of such a system. First, however, a question arises: why are some academics only now coming to worry about faculty development?

Many forces have converged to create such a climate of concern, and several of them call for special attention: the complex response to recent attempts to experiment within the system of higher education, to reform or even to go outside it; demands that institutions and their faculties be held accountable for providing the educational

---

With regard to teaching, the academic culture
is remarkably unreflective. This derives
from the dreary record of many educationists who profess
to train teachers, from the tendency of every profession
to cloak its own processes in mystery as a way
to achieve status, and from the notion that an academic
is valuable for what he knows, rather than
for what he can help other people learn.

---

services needed by students and by the society; and a declining rate of academic mobility, both in terms of movement from one institution to another and advancement within a particular institution.

To start with the last, recall the happy days when academic budgets were growing and departments could seek to develop themselves simply by recruiting talent to fill slots as they became available. An individual professor in those days could readily envision his or her own development in the form of a plump job offer from someplace else. There was a widespread sense that a department was not limited to the staff it already had, nor a professor to the place he or she happened to work. On book jackets many a tenured author was said to be "currently" at a certain college. In this atmosphere the ambitious or dissatisfied could easily seek to leave, rather than to improve, their own departments. Of course, not all professors wanted to move—either to escape a situation or to seek a better salary, new colleagues, or higher prestige. But the possibility affected the academic climate.

That sense of mobility has now faded. Quite apart from issues of academic freedom, tenured professors give renewed thanks for their lifelong security. With eyes on younger faculty, rival unions and associations outbid one another in denouncing quotas on tenure. Recent graduates meanwhile scout for jobs in places they had earlier been taught to scorn. In a time of financial retrenchment, the unkindest cuts are felt by young people who can find no job at all in their fields, and many receive offers only from institutions that have little they had expected in facilities, challenges, and prestige.

However, cutbacks also affect many professors who already have secure and respectable jobs, but who feel less able than before to develop their careers by moving to new places. Nor can departments any longer hope to keep themselves vital, raise their prestige, or enlarge their scope simply by recruiting additional members. And the possibility of leaving an institution or of having new people join it may have been no less important to morale, at least among the enterprising and the disaffected, than the right to keep a job for life. If so, a decline in the sense of mobility may itself have serious effects, quite apart from whatever happens to tenure. We are now faced, at worst, with the prospect of local colleagues growing old together, unable either to add new faces to their company or, individually, to find other places.

Such a caricature omits the possibility that, even if mobility declines to zero, the members of a department or an institution could help one another develop where they are. Although colleges and universities have always encouraged or required their faculty members to develop in some ways, they have seldom provided as much help as they could, and they have widely neglected certain aspects of development altogether. And mobility, though beneficial in many ways, relieved pressure for, and concealed the potential benefits of, faculty development within a given institution. During the era of mobility, neglect of faculty development was harmful, but the loss was concealed; in a time of retrenchment, continued neglect could become profoundly depressing.

The rigors of reform, of course, make clear that only a sophisticated program of faculty development can produce the assent, teach the skills, and provide the support without which even good ideas may fail. Most plans for improving education do not necessarily assume that faculty will develop in new ways but focus instead upon inducing them to work harder. Such plans may rearrange the curriculum or offer relief from it (as in the case of independent study), but they do not necessarily affect a professor's style of learning or kinds of interests.

This oversight has had serious consequences. Faculty can simply sabotage programs they do not like or do not know how to handle. As any educational reformer knows, changes won on paper are often lost in performance. Whether through opposition, disinterest, or inability, professors have reduced many programs to parodies of themselves or to faintly disguised versions of what they were meant to replace. Naturally, this sort of failure leads to depression and cynicism.

In a time of financial shortages and student quiescence, faculty development appears to be the chief method for improving education, or at least a prerequisite to any others; and without a sophisticated network of support for teaching, many improvements simply will not occur. Lacking such necessary support, teachers do not often have the training, motivation, resources, and information that would facilitate better teaching; and as long as they do not, academics will be defensive about departures from basic teaching patterns. In fact, many of the patterns assumed to be a necessary part of college teaching derive in part from anxiety aroused by practicing the art of teaching almost wholly in isolation. That isolation must be broken down so that teachers can learn together how to answer increasingly strong demands for their accountability.

---

**In the past, reformers have often attempted to improve teaching by exhorting professors to rededicate themselves to the task, by providing tips on technique, by readjusting the subject matter, by offering prizes for exemplary performance, and the like. It is hard to estimate the net yield, if any, of these methods. What has not been done is to develop an adequate system of supports resting on a network of new kinds of relationships between a teacher and his or her colleagues, students, administrators, and experts on the processes of learning.**

---

Despite cycles of anti-intellectualism, resentment at the soft life professors are thought to lead, and suspicions of political unreliability, large parts of the American public have long been enchanted by higher education. They have regarded it as the path to economic and social mobility, as a source of culture and of knowledge valuable to society, and in the case of many nostalgic alumni, as the pretext for the best years of their lives. To some extent, the enchantment has recently been shaken.

The story is too complex to untangle here, but the suspicion has grown among taxpayers and alumni that professors are not very effective as teachers—except on behalf of political or cultural radicalism. People suspect that even when effective, education no longer necessarily leads to a good job and that professors enjoy a measure of free time and autonomy denied to most of those who pay their keep. For these and other reasons, people are asking that professors, like others, be held accountable for doing a good job—in this case on behalf of students and of society. This pressure can take specific shape, for example, in the efforts of officials on the state level, as well as within large institutions, to discover what faculty members do with their time, to estimate the cost-effectiveness of academic departments, and to evaluate the teaching performance of individual professors.

The decline of academic mobility, the lessons learned from attempts at reform, the call for accountability—each helps to explain the current interest in faculty development. Probably the main reason for supporting a program of faculty development, however, is the effect it could have on the quality of teaching and thus on the morale of both professors and students.

In the past, reformers have often attempted to improve teaching by exhorting professors to rededicate themselves to the task, by providing tips on technique, by readjusting the subject matter, by offering prizes for exemplary performance, and the like. It is hard to estimate the net yield, if any, of these methods. What has not been done is to develop an adequate system of supports resting on a network of new kinds of relationships between a teacher and his or her colleagues, students, administrators, and experts on the processes of learning.

# 2

# Kinds
# of
# Reform

Why some old devices to encourage good teaching don't work, and what strategies may be used to achieve substantial improvements in the quality of college teaching. Some practical and reasonable departures from current practice can substantially enhance the professionalization of teaching.

$P$LANS FOR REFORM THAT CARRY A COMMON LABEL ARE
often treated as if they were all directed toward a common goal, reflected similar assumptions, and even could be substituted for one
another. In fact, certain plans will probably not lead to much progress, while others require a context of other reforms to be fully successful. Building a system of support for teaching is no less complex
than creating an audience for the arts while supporting their practice and training young performers and artists. The task calls for a
variety of initiatives during several stages of development. So, too,
does faculty development.

The following list of kinds of reform omits or touches lightly on
some valuable possibilities, and those it does include could be
grouped in other ways. Some kinds are far harder to introduce than
others. Not all are appropriate to all institutions. And some reforms,
while useful in themselves, may serve to divert energy from more
far-reaching methods. In any case, the following list will both illustrate the scope of the task and introduce the sections that follow—
sections that deal with particular aspects of a program for faculty
development.

## Rewards for Individual Initiative

UNDER STRAIN, A SYSTEM THAT DEPENDS on individual striving
for recognition turns first to such devices as the committee that
praises good teaching, the teaching award, and even to talk about
allowing people more time for their pedagogical duties. Although
well-administered teaching awards have given recognition to de-
serving professors, one can argue that their net effect has been to
ease the conscience of most faculty about the quality of the teaching
the prize committees do not examine. Meanwhile, the existence of
awards has reinforced the view some faculty hold that "teaching" is
necessary mainly in survey courses and probably violates habits of
mind necessary for sound scholarship. Even when nonrecipients
have more sophisticated reactions, the existence of a prize offers little incentive for special effort except to those who are already exceptionally good. Most important, prizes give no help to a teacher

who wants to improve but doesn't know how, or thinks he or she knows how but needs help in doing so. A more fruitful way to recognize the best teachers would be to ease their normal burdens and give them a serious role in working with other less accomplished teachers.

As for study groups that judiciously stress the continuing importance of teaching, their reports are quite harmless except when mistaken for action. Allowing extraordinary performance as a teacher to make up for a certain delay or eccentricity in publishing is perhaps good in itself; but again, it has no effect on the great majority of teachers. Besides, tenure committees begrudge such allowances, as we see in case after case where teachers are widely praised but not kept.

Improving the quality of teaching through rewards for individual initiative may also involve arrangements for allowing professors to lighten their loads or to get away for awhile on a sabbatical or other leave. Faculty often assume that development necessarily requires withdrawal—a wish expressed, for example, in fantasies about a cabin in the woods or simply an obscure carrel in the library. Most faculty are frustrated by demands outside the classroom, especially by committee meetings, and some are so heavily burdened that they have neither time nor energy for improvement.

The present financial stringency allows little hope that these burdens will be lightened, but professors could seek relief from what they are currently doing, if not by periodic withdrawals, at least by helping to change the content of their jobs. If the institutions were governed by means more efficient and satisfying than the present welter of committees, if demands leading to make-work research were balanced by other means for achieving recognition, or if professors were asked to lecture only when appropriate material was not available in print or other media, very substantial fractions of the work week could be salvaged.

The most effective reward for individual initiative in teaching is probably official recognition by the college in the form of promotion, salary increases, and other marks of status, and this will require clearer guidelines and fuller information. Although department chairmen and tenure committees do pay attention to the quality of teaching, they do not always have reliable evidence about teaching effectiveness. Nor do they regularly make clear, in advance, what styles of teaching they approve or what weight they will assign to whatever evidence they do collect. Widespread vagueness about criteria, evidence, and emphasis undoubtedly reduces the incentive rhetoric provides about the value of teaching.

## Accountability

A SKEPTIC HAS SAID that the accountability movement consists of people who do not teach telling professors what to do but not otherwise helping them do it. In contrast to rewards for individual initiative, accountability relies on controls by students (often regarded as consumers), by deans (management), by trustees and regents (the board of directors), and possibly even by accrediting associations (the regulatory agency). In some ways, these pressure groups can assist faculty development, especially when they force professors to define their goals more clearly, learn what various programs cost, help to evaluate their benefits, and weigh alternatives. To be sure, the value of some very good programs may defy prior description and even be hard to evaluate after the fact. Nonetheless, professors could probably improve their work by defining the criteria in terms of which participants in a program, and observers of it, can judge its success.

---

**Oddly enough, most professors are not given
enough occasions to discuss either their teaching
or their professional development. Researchers have found
many faculty willing to examine what they are trying to do,
how they got into it, what the difficulties are,
and how well they are doing.
They want to talk about ways in which
they would like to change
or have their institutions change.**

---

However, the accountability movement contains some disturbing possibilities. Outsiders may impose inappropriate criteria that fail adequately to assess a program or that warp it. Such a possibility may seem remote, but many other important changes in higher education, such as the disturbances of the 1960s and the sharp tightening of the job market, were not widely foreseen. Associations and governing bodies in higher education have seriously discussed accountability, not always with sufficient awareness of the difficulty of defining clear and relevant criteria or making fair, reliable, and nonintrusive measurements of educational outcomes.

At present, teachers are seldom able to specify how much knowledge students have gained from a particular course, as measured by tests at the start and finish, much less to compare such a measurement to the abilities of students involved. If this were done, and if the necessary apparatus did not itself distort the process of learning, "value added" would be a powerful measure of teaching effectiveness. In advanced courses, especially, it is difficult enough to measure what students know or can do at any given point without trying to make a comparison. But the movement assumes that one can compare and then weigh the gain according to a valid measure of individual abilities, determining finally how much of the advance is attributable to the course and making sure that everything the course has done is reflected in the tests. To create a fair and reliable measure of the effectiveness of even a single course is an objective worth seeking, but in general this objective is far from being achieved.

Unfortunately, it is no less difficult to evaluate the process of teaching than to measure the outcomes, especially when that process is itself affected by the presence of outsiders whose official judgments will affect the career of the teacher. Such a system of evaluation differs sharply from an invited visit by a trusted colleague or outside observer who reports only to the teacher and only for the purpose of helping the teacher improve his or her work. The sense of intrusiveness can be reduced by asking students who have attended the class to fill out questionnaires about the quality of the teaching. However, a system of term-end evaluations, whatever its bureaucratic uses, offers students little training as constructive critics of teaching, provides information only when the course is over, and fails adequately to support the teacher's attempts to improve.

As in the case of rewards for individual initiatives, the accountability movement suggests some devices that may assist faculty development; but neither of these methods, by itself, can possibly take the place of other methods described below.

## Assisted Self-Study

LIKE ACCOUNTABILITY, THE USE OF CONSULTANTS gives a key role to people outside the faculty, but in this case to helpers rather than to official evaluators. Some administrators in higher education make good use of consultants, but programs for faculty development, where they exist at all, have not taken full advantage of what outside experts can offer. Rather than bringing in consultants, faculty may insist that the money could better be spent on professorial salaries, say, or on the library. In general, outsiders concerned with faculty development make most progress when, as in the case of the Danforth workshops, they have their own money. A few training programs have helped a small fraction of college teachers. Typically, this fraction is pictured as a catalytic agent, but since teachers do not usually come in direct contact with the teaching of others, the reaction seldom has a place in which to occur.

At worst, faculty development programs can use consultants, as colleges have often used self-study groups, to acknowledge a problem with a tolerable degree of self-criticism while hoping that the problem will disappear or at least become a bore. Among themselves, consultants hotly debate a variety of "intervention strategies," but even when they see what needs to be done and explain it clearly, their brilliant analysis hardly ensures that their plan will be adopted. Consultants come and go, but the faculty remain. Only if they become involved can a program succeed. One mode of involvement is to ask faculty to help with research on higher education on their own campuses.

Oddly enough, most professors are not given enough occasions to discuss either their teaching or their professional development. Researchers have found many faculty willing to examine what they are trying to do, how they got into it, what the difficulties are, and how well they are doing. They want to talk about ways in which they would like to change or have their institutions change. A knowledgeable outside interviewer often elicits material that professors say they have not discussed with anyone, except perhaps their spouses. If a large number of faculty are interviewed, they may begin to discuss the experience with others and to compare notes, and the process intensifies.

If the team of researchers reports to members of the faculty and perhaps to others in the community, professors may discover they share problems and aspirations they seldom discuss with their colleagues. In this sense, a report may give faculty a new perspective on the academic culture in which they all participate and, with further work, may even help to modify that culture. Combined with various small group sessions, this approach to faculty development may not only loosen the fixity of academic culture but give faculty a forum in which to discuss issues not ordinarily raised.

Outsiders can extend their effect by training people on campus to assume consulting and research roles. The requirements of interviewing overlap with those of teaching: the researcher must learn to listen closely, to intuit assumptions, to discuss the concerns lying behind attitudes, and to follow a line of inquiry. Once the process is begun, colleagues may interview one another. They can do so most fruitfully across departmental lines—a situation in which people are less defensive and interviewers can learn something about another discipline. Likewise, faculty may learn how to study their students, in particular their styles of curiosity and learning, their viewpoints on the college, and the interplay between the developmental tasks of late adolescence and the work of the classroom. In part, information on these themes is available in the literature on student development, but a study of students would involve faculty more directly, yield fresh information, and offer a shared task for a number of professors, who would naturally discuss the work as it proceeded. The value of such a study lies as much in the breadth of faculty participation as in the scientific purity of its findings.

Faculty generally assume they already know what students are like: after all, they were students themselves, they deal with students every week, and they may have adolescents in the family. However, a student often will not talk as openly to a teacher as to a sympathetic person with whom he or she is not otherwise involved. Outside an authority relationship, students are as eager as faculty to tell about their ways of learning and living, and many professors can learn how to listen, respond supportively, and acquire the necessary skills to study students.

## Programs on Teaching

A PROGRAM OF ASSISTED SELF-STUDY encourages people on a campus to discover one another, clarify their goals, and approach their work in a new spirit. Unless adroitly handled, however, interviewing faculty and students and reporting on the data may increase suspicion and misunderstanding on a campus. And even if a program is well conducted, it may lead to little more than what participants describe as a good catharsis. To the extent that the faculty increase their self-awareness about the kind of teaching they would most like to do, and the kinds of academic relationships they would like to create, this self-awareness may produce a renewed sense of frustration unless institutions create structures in which they can work toward these ambitions. Professors who are interviewed may discuss their feelings with colleagues and may try to improve their own courses, but only a campus program on teaching can move self-awareness into shared action.

A thoroughgoing campus program on teaching should include the following:
- regular, detailed observations of and discussions about teaching by colleagues, visitors, specialists, and students;
- a widespread, disciplined sharing of knowledge about learning

as an activity, based on the experience of faculty and students, the expertise of researchers, and written autobiographical accounts of learning;

● the systematic training of graduate students, as part of their normal program, in skills useful to a future professor;

● the establishment of a campus teaching institute to coordinate and assist all of these activities;

● the creation of a new contract between professors and their students that would provide various ways to certify student mastery other than requiring a teacher to grade his or her own students and would urge more elaborate faculty assessments of student work for the sole use of each student.

---

**To the extent that the faculty increase
their self-awareness about the kind of teaching they would
most like to do, and the kinds of academic relationships
they would like to create, this self-awareness
may produce a renewed sense of frustration
unless institutions create structures in which
they can work toward these ambitions.
Professors who are interviewed may discuss their feelings
with colleagues and may try to improve
their own courses, but only a campus program on teaching
can move self-awareness into shared action.**

---

Some would say the reform we've described represents the professionalization of college teaching—its advance to the stage reached by the world of research and publication. In many ways, this is a useful description, so long as we remember that teaching is inherently an unusual profession. Certainly professionalization requires relief from the teacher's current role as double-agent, both educator and grader of the same student; certainly it calls for systematic training in sharing as well as in acquiring knowledge; and certainly it calls for a rich response about the quality of the practice.

### Grants for Teaching

IN ADDITION TO CAMPUS PROGRAMS ON TEACHING, inventive professors need access to resources to help them prepare, conduct, and evaluate special courses and programs. A radical disparity in scale has developed, at least at the more high-powered institutions, between grants and contracts available for research, usually from outside sources, and funds available for the improvement of teaching; and in spite of sharp cutbacks in support for some lines of research, the disparity persists. With regard to facilities available, if not always with regard to personal salaries, professors with substantial research grants have lived in a different world from their colleagues who are essentially teachers. If a fraction of research funds were diverted to professors who want to create special projects in teaching, the improvement in the quality of education would far outweigh the loss to research. Many good research projects have found support; special projects in teaching hardly ever do.

## Intellectual Mobility

TOGETHER WITH THE CAMPUS PROGRAM ON teaching sketched above, the creation of new structures for instruction and research alongside what is now a departmental monopoly would facilitate intellectual mobility. True, the monopoly is occasionally softened by joint appointments, ad hoc degree committees, interdisciplinary programs for undergraduates, and research institutes that draw on more than a single department. Generally, however, academic life is governed by a territorial metaphor about knowledge, with all of knowledge fenced into a patchwork of fields, and each professor restricted more or less to one of them. Over the years there has been a lot of talk about the virtues of crossing the fences and redrawing the boundaries, but little has been done to engender and sustain a necessarily demanding kind of work. Some professors appear to regard becoming involved in work that goes beyond a single discipline as taboo breaking; others use the term "cross-disciplinary" as if it were a mark of automatic virtue.

Most professors, however, probably distrust both attitudes and would be happy to think afresh about how they can more fruitfully associate with one another. In response, institutions would do well to help them associate more flexibly than they can now, and, in particular, to share in the work of several units, without necessarily being permanently attached to all of them or hired by any single one. But before discussing organizational problems, let us think of college teaching as a profession, in part by briefly comparing it with the research professions and with professions such as law or medicine.

# 3

## Teaching
## as
## a
## Performing
## Art

Teaching, unlike research and publishing, remains very much a private professional act, rarely open to collegial scrutiny. Effective teaching remains a stepchild in the hierarchy of academic goals and values. It could be greatly improved by opening up the process to sensible and substantive criticism.

A PROFESSOR WHO REMARKS OF A COLLEAGUE THAT HE OR she is a "performer" rarely intends the remark as a compliment. On the academic scene the word mainly suggests a striving for flashy effects rather than for truth, a display of oneself at the expense of the subject, or a pandering to the presumed taste of late adolescents. Most professors are eager to avoid the charge of flashiness, preferring to think of themselves as transmitters of knowledge and skills, as people with material to be got through, ground to cover, points to convey. They also dislike the imputation that they are merely "performing" a script written out in advance. They want to respond sensitively to student questions and contributions during classes. Taken either way, most professors do not want to be regarded as performers.

Nonetheless, teaching can be seen as a performing art. Like drama or the dance, it happens and then, except in memory, is gone. This has very far-reaching consequences. Few professors make reputations as teachers beyond their own campuses, and even a teacher's local reputation is mostly hearsay. Unlike many performers, the teacher almost always works alone: a course may have more than one lecturer, or may include a staff of subordinates, but seldom do peers interact, as it were, on the platform. However, as a performing artist, the teacher escapes criticism to an astonishing degree. In fact, the teacher is in the remarkable position of judging his or her own audience, and he does so not only to their faces but in permanent form for the use of outsiders. In return, the teacher seldom knows how good a job he has done, much less how well he is doing at any given moment, though much of his professional satisfaction depends on how effectively he teaches.

A comparison between teaching and publishing will clarify the situation. Younger teachers, especially, are told *what* to teach to help satisfy the department's supposed need to offer a full range of courses and to provide introductory ones for large numbers of students; yet *how well* they teach is often cloaked in the privacy of the classroom. In contrast, nobody tells a professor what he should study in his research, but the results, when published, are open to the scrutiny of his colleagues. In teaching, a professor is called upon to judge his audience; in research, he is judged by it—and judges the work of others in his field. A teacher holds an audience for a semester if he or she is lucky, whereas a scholar through his writing builds a reputation over decades among readers who include his peers in learning.

Such a comparison briefly highlights two unhappy circumstances that teachers now suffer. First, a teacher must rely for response to his teaching almost solely on a captive audience: he has little or no help from trained observers of teaching and very little from colleagues. Second, students are seldom deliberately trained, as part of their general education, to assess the quality of the teaching they encounter, to observe the process of their own learning, or to work more effectively with groups, such as classes, or authority figures, such as professors. To be sure, some colleges and universities have been graced by student course guides based upon questionnaires submitted by samples of students enrolled in each course. While these are better than nothing, especially when the campus is too large for a student to rely simply on his friends for advice, course guides do not call for enough criticism by a sufficiently wide group.

---

**A teacher must rely for response to his teaching
almost solely on a captive audience: he has little
or no help from trained observers of teaching
and very little from colleagues.
Students are seldom deliberately trained, as part of their
general education, to assess the quality
of the teaching they encounter, to observe the process
of their own learning, or to work
more effectively with groups, such as classes,
or authority figures, such as professors.**

---

Some student judgments are of course perfunctory. When asked about a teacher, as when asked about a movie, some will say little more than "he's disorganized" or "he's really great," but the very poverty of the response suggests that the process of education ought to include a sharpening of judgment about the process itself. Given opportunities to reflect on the teaching they encounter, students may discover how to take better advantage of it, as well as how to give advice about its improvement. And when their judgment is taken seriously, the quality of that judgment is most likely to improve.

To regard teaching as a performing art is to see that it not only reverses ordinary patterns of criticism but that it also occurs in a sort of pedagogical amateurs' hour. In a profession otherwise notable for its requirements, prerequisites, hurdles, and elaborate dossiers, skills needed for effective teaching are treated off-handedly, as if mere imitation of graduate school models were perhaps enough. When observers urge deliberate training in these skills, the defensive reactions go somewhat as follows: nobody knows how to train teachers; graduate students can easily pick it up on their own; all they need is to do unto others what's been done unto them; most graduate students do get experience as teaching assistants; and besides, there's not enough time as it is for "substantive" learning, much less all these "frills."

> **Most faculty receive their professional training
> at institutions primarily dedicated to advanced
> research in science and scholarship.
> The models available to graduate students
> are the subject-matter specialists who teach them....
> Yet most of the undergraduates they will teach
> will not plan academic careers.**

Juxtaposed like this, the reactions suggest a certain tension among various strands of the argument. In fact, it is probably not an exaggeration to say that the present disjunction between the emphasis in graduate training and the work done by most college teachers is a formula for occupational schizophrenia.

Most faculty receive their professional training at institutions primarily dedicated to advanced research in science and scholarship. The models available to graduate students are the subject-matter specialists who teach them. Graduate students in turn are rewarded both by the faculty and their student peers for carefully exploring scientific or scholarly interests. Yet most of the undergraduates they will teach will not plan academic careers. And most faculty members work within an intellectual and cultural atmosphere less highly charged than at the university where they received their graduate training. Caught in this conflict, professors at state colleges and even junior colleges struggle to help their institutions acquire university status, regardless of the resources available or the specific needs of the students.

Further, some professors fail to acquire a broad sense of competence, in part because they have a trained incapacity to inquire vigorously beyond an area of specialization. And this intellectual parochialism has dubious consequences for faculty governance and curricular planning. Faculty so limited are simply unequipped to frame a program that responds to a student's own level of conceptual, affective, and esthetic understanding.

Every profession must both recruit and train new members, and provide a service to outsiders. In some professions these two tasks are largely separated. Most physicians do not teach in the medical schools, nor are the best law schools staffed primarily by practicing attorneys. A teacher in a conservatory may show special interest in a student who plans to teach, but the teacher does not necessarily value that student more than a talented young performer. The same applies in a business school or in any graduate program from which a majority of students enter nonacademic jobs.

However, in academic fields professors often show the keenest in-

---

A teacher preoccupied with passing the discipline along to future academic specialists may neglect students who have other uses for the knowledge. And a discipline required only to extend itself rather than to confront the questions, problems, data, or methods of outsiders may suffer from conceptual inbreeding.

---

terest in recruiting students who will become academics and thereby perpetuate their own specialties. In one sense this is commendable: certainly a professor who doubts the value of his or her own field ought not to teach it, and if the field does engage the professor's best energies he or she naturally wants it to thrive. However, two problems arise. A teacher preoccupied with passing the discipline along to future academic specialists may neglect students who have other uses for the knowledge. And a discipline required only to extend itself rather than to confront the questions, problems, data, or methods of outsiders may suffer from conceptual inbreeding. In this case, the discipline comes to insist on its mysteries, special language, and preoccupations, on a style of initiating recruits and loftily giving advice.

To be sure, all professions are based on specialized knowledge, but whereas the work of most professionals is to apply that knowledge and provide a service for clients, teachers are called upon to transfer to others the very knowledge that sets them apart. A physician is expected to cure his or her patient, not to initiate the patient into the complexities of medical knowledge. Like other professionals, academics may put their knowledge to practical use, but unlike the others, their main work—except for those few professors who primarily do research—is to help other people, generally younger, to acquire the knowledge the teacher already has or can find.

Teaching might thus be defined as the profession required to give away its own secrets, a performing art that should reveal its own workings and articulate its tacit assumptions. Teachers are thus subject to unusual demands: not only must they put on a show, as it were; they must tell what they are doing and help the audience learn to do it too. Between these two demands there is an often unacknowledged tension. Instead of learning to make use of this tension, many teachers relieve it simply by neglecting the responsibility to help students become self-reflective about the way they learn, which presumably includes consideration of the work done by professors. As a result, teaching remains the performing art least aided by the benefits of criticism.

# 4

# Knowledge About Learning

Self-reflectiveness about the processes of teaching and learning can become a viable instrument for teacher and student alike. Such awareness is rarely present today. An institutionalized intellectual concern for the nature of learning may represent the last remaining bit of common culture in the modern, diffused multiversity.

T HE WAY TEACHERS REACT TO STUDENT COURSE EVALUA-
tions suggests that knowledge about the process of teaching and
learning is not very widely shared. When student evaluations are
merely advisory and only the professor sees the completed questionnaires, the faculty is likely to support those evaluations. Many are
curious about how students really regard the course, and the privacy of the evaluations lessens opposition. We find another response, however, in places where student evaluations have a serious effect on faculty careers. Professors rightly criticize the limitations, indeed sometimes the outright crudity, of the questionnaires
and other instruments used for evaluating courses. Some faculty
also oppose evaluation on the grounds that students do not know
enough to evaluate reliably and wisely the work of a professional.
They argue not that the students are biased but that they are relatively ignorant about what a teacher should be doing, careless or
awkward about describing what he or she in fact does, and unreflective about the intricacies of how they, as students, respond. Professors are often wary of developing these points in public, but they
hold them more tenaciously as the student judgments matter more.
In addition, a number of students appear to share these doubts
about their judgment, even when they are not satisfied with
a particular course: after all, the professor is the expert.

Noting this self-doubt on the part of some students and granting
the argument made by some faculty, we may either conclude that
course evaluations should not be taken very seriously, or pause and
ask whether teachers might not have a responsibility to help students learn how to assess what each of them is doing. If students
can be taught to describe, analyze, and even evaluate a complex
poem, an historical configuration, or a psychological syndrome, similar skills could be applied to the process that leads to these accom-
plishments. Some faculty might argue that if the student absorbs the

subject matter satisfactorily, he or she should not be diverted by paying attention to the process through which this happens. Some might even say that not only do students lose time through this form of self-consciousness and pedagogical observation, they may be paralyzed by their own divided attention.

But students in fact are conscious, to a widely varying degree, of how they learn and what helps them, of stages they pass through in reacting to things that are new. This knowledge does not necessarily owe much to the faculty or to organized discussions among students. But the very challenge of confronting so much material that is new in kind induces at least some students to reflect on their processes of learning. Self-reflectiveness about methods of teaching, however, is not strongly encouraged by faculty culture. This is ironic because most scholars are self-conscious about the methods of their scholarship, whether those of biochemistry, social inquiry, or literary criticism. In fact, many debates properly revolve around not the substance of what is found, but the methods by which it was derived, especially, of course, in fields where the finding cannot easily be

---

**We are badly served by a failure to distinguish
between learning as an outcome and learning as an activity.
The distinction may seem superfluous,
because if students are active in learning,
sooner or later they will
have learned something; but if the institution shows
an interest only in what has been acquired,
students may neglect to think about the methods
of its acquisition. Ideally, students would be taught
to observe both the process and outcomes
of learning and to relate one to the other.**

---

demonstrated. To outsiders, this methodological preoccupation may appear as ridiculous as the man who never got where he wanted to go because he kept arguing about how to travel. At worst, self-reflectiveness can become a substitute for doing or concluding anything, but at best it is indispensable to the progress of disciplines.

In a similar spirit, professors and students could gain by reflecting regularly upon the process by which they think, teach, and learn about these subjects. The history of science traces this process, as do intellectual and cultural history and, in a different way, the study of human development. Within the university, however, it is not enough to study the past or the completed processes of learning. Universities have an obligation to help their staff and students monitor their own intellectual history as it is being made—in its failure as well as in its accomplishment—reflecting upon learning and the resources that help it occur.

Self-reflectiveness about learning and teaching is difficult, as each person is caught between immersion in and examination of a process. But self-reflectiveness in higher education is also discouraged by the tendency of professionals to mystify what they do; the dependency of students who do not wish to take responsibility for their own learning, to confront their own confusions, or to challenge authority; the prevalence both of rigorous but over-generalized "learning theories" and self-aggrandizing, romantic images of learning; and the lack of means through which the process of education could itself be routinely studied by those directly involved. Ordinarily, institutions do not provide structures that would encourage people to share their knowledge of teaching and learning, or to develop it through discussion that would help other people, less advanced, learn what is known and reflect on their own experience. Some professors may talk among themselves about their classroom methods and their intellectual interests; students, about some of their experiences of learning, not confined, of course, to the formal curriculum. But where is there a campus culture of intense self-reflectiveness about learning? Finally, we are badly served by a failure to distinguish between learning as an outcome and learning as an activity. The distinction may seem superfluous, because if students are active in learning, sooner or later they will have learned something; but if the institution shows an interest only in what has been acquired, students may neglect to think about the methods of its acquisition. Ideally, students would be taught to observe both the process and outcomes of learning and to relate one to the other.

As the university has flown apart into a set of loosely related specialties, one of the few interests its members could have in common, apart from concern for their collective welfare, is knowledge about teaching and learning: this in fact could become the common culture the multiversity and sometimes even the liberal arts colleges now lack. If faculty developed the same degree of self-reflectiveness about their common activity of teaching as each of them has about his or her particular field, they would be able to share their experiences and thus enliven their work as teachers.

# 5

## Training
## Future
## Professors

Few graduate schools prepare their students for teaching in any practical sense, leaving classroom performance largely to chance. A new teaching practicum, new teaching degrees, and the encouragement of intellectual work directed toward the classroom are some devices to upgrade current teaching effectiveness.

GRADUATE STUDENTS AS WELL AS PROFESSORS CAN BENEFIT
from disciplined knowledge about the process of learning. As teaching assistants, they receive some response to their work, unless they
are insensitive to the way students react. Like all students they have
some knowledge of how they go about learning. However, except in
a small number of pioneering programs, the evaluation of teaching
is haphazard in form and unsophisticated in content. Although dedicated to learning, graduate schools study everything except the
ways in which their own students learn.

Since the PhD is the union card for undergraduate teaching, at
least in most four-year colleges, graduate schools leave the impression that they do indeed prepare their students for teaching. But in
general, most departments and schools act as if they believe that a
graduate student who knows "the field" reasonably well and has
written an acceptable dissertation can certainly teach. In recom-
mending a graduate student for his first job, a professor may write
that although he has not personally observed the applicant conduct
classes, he has every confidence in the applicant's ability to teach.
After all, to the extent that teaching is mainly the transmission of
knowledge, all a practitioner needs, in addition to a reasonable command of the discipline, is an audible voice: the students will tune in
and receive whatever they can.

When students begin to complain and demand something better,
when deans require department chairmen or other professors to assess the teaching performance of a colleague, these evaluators may
nonetheless infer quality of teaching largely from conversations
with colleagues, remarks by favored students, and the quality of
published works. Many departments simply assert that working as a
teaching assistant gives valuable experience, at least to those not
bright or energetic enough to secure a research assistantship. Meeting weekly with a section of somebody else's large lecture course,
however, sparring with students about what will be on the test, trying to explain what the lectures meant or conducting a routine lab—
none of this prepares future professors for a less hectic or alienated
style of teaching. Occasionally a dean or a department official may
offer a seminar on teaching (such as those for teaching assistants in

freshman English), but few such courses are taken as seriously as the "real" curriculum; and few offer closely supervised experience rather than tips, academic bookkeeping procedures, and generalities.

Most academics resist the education school model that forces elementary and secondary school teachers to sit through various lectures on theory, methods, problems, and the history of education—all to earn their certificates or qualify for pay raises. Some recent work at leading schools of education has been exciting, but the general level of thought and training in this field has not aroused much interest or respect. In recoil from a didactic approach, some people who want to reform teaching often call for the identification of master teachers, but they rarely explain how such people can be identified or teach others to teach. Mere imitation is not necessarily a useful style of learning.

Neither approach to teacher education—the TA (teaching assistantship) system, which initiates graduate students under the worst of conditions, nor the didactic model used frequently in the training of teachers—offers much hope. One alternative might be to add an additional stage at the end of the regular PhD program for the pedagogical training of those who plan a career in teaching. Another al-

---

**Observers have noticed that many teachers in higher education, especially outside the elite universities, publish little or nothing; that people can learn to interpret and explain books or research reports without having written a dissertation; and that the longer students are exposed to the practice of narrow research, the more snobbish they may become about teaching and the less capable of doing it.**

---

ternative begins by subtracting the last stage of the existing program—the dissertation. In effect, the latter plan offers as a formal option what would otherwise be regarded as a mark of procrastination, the "ABD" (all but dissertation) status.

To consider the latter proposal first, observers have noticed that many teachers in higher education, especially outside the elite universities, publish little or nothing; that people can learn to interpret and explain books or research reports without having written a dissertation; and that the longer students are exposed to the practice of narrow research, the more snobbish they may become about teaching and the less capable of doing it. Why not, then, simply offer some students special preparation for teaching, recognize the status of those who honorably finish all but the dissertation, and award them a master of philosophy, a doctor of arts, or some other teaching degree? Clearly, the holders of such degrees would not be hired over PhDs for jobs involving research, but they might be welcome in positions in which publication is not necessarily expected.

This plan has several obvious advantages. Surely we can no longer rely exclusively on a graduate degree program that trains future teachers for a kind of work many of them will seldom or never do, a program that suggests in a hundred ways that what they *will* do is inferior to research, fails to prepare them for their jobs, and nonetheless drags out their degree programs. To the extent that a doctor of arts program not merely subtracts the dissertation requirement but adds supervised experience in teaching, it might well prepare its graduates to respond sensitively to, and work imaginatively with, their students.

---

**The doctor of arts program has several
limitations. The degree's prestige would inevitably lag
behind that of the PhD, except perhaps
in community colleges; and at a time when several fields
suffer a surplus of PhDs, holders of the DA degree
might be pushed to the margins
of the job market. Nor would
the new program significantly change
the graduate schools if candidates for the DA
were tolerated as a lower caste, less devoted
than PhD candidates to the "pursuit of truth"
and the "pushing back of frontiers,"
prepared only to harvest fields
explored, claimed, and cultivated by others.**

---

Even if adopted far more widely than at present, however, the doctor of arts program has several limitations. The degree's prestige would inevitably lag behind that of the PhD, except perhaps in community colleges; and at a time when several fields suffer a surplus of PhDs, holders of the DA degree might be pushed to the margins of the job market. Nor would the new program significantly change the graduate schools if candidates for the DA were tolerated as a lower caste, less devoted than PhD candidates to the "pursuit of truth" and the "pushing back of frontiers," prepared only to harvest fields explored, claimed, and cultivated by others.

Another proposal is that future teachers be given not less but more training than those who prefer doing research to teaching undergraduates. Here the model that comes to mind is the internship in medicine, during which a doctor, after finishing medical school, puts his knowledge to the test by work with patients. Similarly, a candidate for a super-PhD would meet the present degree requirements and then do further work appropriate for those who wish to teach. This plan has the merit of recognizing that to teach is not simply to transfer knowledge. It has the disadvantage of extending what is already, in many cases, an unnecessarily and depressingly long graduate training, and of continuing to require everybody to present a so-called original contribution to knowledge. Moreover, the plan for adding a year of pedagogical training after the normal

PhD program is completed not only defers entry into a "real" academic career, but what is worse, it perpetuates the split between specialist training in a discipline and pedagogical training. Only after the one is finished would the other even begin.

Ideally, the PhD program should do what it already claims to do: prepare its graduates for effective college teaching. Since this degree serves as an entree to the most prestigious teaching jobs, one might expect that graduate schools would explain what they are doing to train students for the kind of work most of them will actually spend the greater portion of their time doing, and if the schools

---

**Graduate schools should broaden the traditional notion of what counts as an original contribution to knowledge. Suitably defined, this phrase can encourage comparative or critical analyses of what is already known, syntheses generated by questions not commonly raised within a single specialty, and even creative work such as the academy routinely assesses but rarely produces. Likewise, originality might flourish more easily for some students in producing several major papers rather than a single monograph or dissertation.**

---

are not doing enough, say what new efforts they will make.

Such new efforts should meet the following criteria: they should occur within the normal span of the PhD program; they should involve all graduate students who plan to teach college students for a substantial part of their time; they should offer practical experience, not merely lectures about teaching; the experience should include close supervision, response from several sources, and a structure for sharing knowledge about learning; schools should make it possible for students to build up a formal record of teaching performance, as part of their dossiers; students should receive credit for essays and even for a dissertation that draws together or interprets knowledge in an original way, as well as for highly specialized research projects.

One arrangement that meets all these criteria is the teaching practicum for graduate students. At worst this could degenerate into a fancy name for the old teaching assistantship, but at best it could give each future professor a chance to experiment with various modes of teaching; to monitor his or her own performance on videotape, either alone or in the company of a master teacher, a graduate student, or anyone else who might be helpful; to study the learning styles of undergraduates, both in the literature and in interviews with students; to practice working on a subject he or she knows nothing about, as an exercise in curiosity and the logic of discovery; to help plan courses as well as work in them; and to collabo-rate in teaching with fellow students, teachers in other fields, and people from outside academic life.

Often proposed before, at least in minimal form, the teaching practicum has met a number of roadblocks. More frequently than not, the practicum has been conceived as a special program, sup-ported by outside funds and largely cut off from the serious work of disciplinary research. It has been dependent on the supervision of a small number of senior faculty or even a single professor whose own priorities may undercut a concern for teaching.

Institutions are unlikely to take the teaching practicum seriously unless the support for it comes from the general budget. Outside funds can help, especially at the beginning; but viable practicum programs will require their own budgetary lines, distinct from those of conventional graduate school activities. They also will require the participation of at least some faculty drawn from, or acting within, the several departments. If a program devoted to the preparation of teachers were cut off from those already teaching, the graduate stu-dent would lose an important resource, and the faculty a useful way of renewing their own skills and expanding their range. Young teachers in the practicum may benefit little from those professors who prefer other work to teaching, practice only a limited range of pedagogical styles, or lack disciplined knowledge of how to help stu-dents develop skills useful in teaching; but skillful and self-reflective teachers on the regular faculty could take the major role, aided by an auxiliary staff of experts on learning and teaching.

A word about timing. Whereas graduate students usually hold teaching assistantships while spending a half or more of their time on their own studies, a teaching practicum might be most effective if blocks of time were provided during which other demands would not distract the participants. Not only should the period be free from courses; it should not fall directly before orals or similar rites of pas-sage. During a typical practicum period, students might team-teach in one course or program as well as plan and prepare for another. Meanwhile they would monitor and discuss their own work, that of other graduate students, and that of professors. They would experi-ment with a variety of styles and methods.

In addition to developing the teaching practicum, graduate schools should broaden the traditional notion of what counts as an original contribution to knowledge. Suitably defined, this phrase can encourage comparative or critical analyses of what is already known, syntheses generated by questions not commonly raised with-in a single specialty, and even creative work such as the academy routinely assesses but rarely produces. Likewise, originality might flourish more easily for some students in producing several major papers rather than a single monograph or dissertation. The avail-ability of these alternatives might help to strengthen general re-search capacity as well as future teaching.

Neglect and distortion of undergraduate teaching are caused not so much by the widespread emphasis on research as by the narrow-ing of research rewards to what can most easily be published in dis-ciplinary journals. Research ought to be done for the benefit of the researcher's audience: when the audience consists of colleagues, one kind of research is appropriate. But to draw on a field for the benefit of a wider audience is an equally demanding kind of work:

intelligent nonspecialists and students who will not become apprentices—which is to say, most people who take courses in a field—call upon a teacher's powers of synthesis and breadth of scholarly imagination.

For many people in a discipline, rewards come from others inside the guild. The concepts originated or elaborated by the discipline generate a special vocabulary, and as it strays further from the common language of educated people, converse with outsiders leads to the awkwardness and delay of translation or to the condescension normal in cults. One of the few reasons insiders in the academ-

---

In academic life, a bargain is struck
by which we gain a standard to meet,
an identity to adopt, and colleagues
to quarrel with, but we may suffer
a degree of isolation within the structure
thus created. Undergraduate teaching
must be directed beyond the field.
We must either treat students as if
they were all protospecialists,
or widen the programs for preparing teachers
so they learn to organize their thoughts around questions
students actually have. PhD programs
can accommodate the latter alternative
much more fully by including the teaching
practicum and encouraging intellectual work directed
at the challenges of the classroom
as well as the referees of scholarly journals.

---

ic world talk to others is to recruit students to the field; another, to impress taxpayers with the value of possible spin-offs; and a third, by no means the least important, to justify faculty salaries. Apart from such motives as these, however, disciplines tend to be autotelic and self-contained: they talk with themselves.

If a given discipline has no message for those outside itself, it should probably not offer courses to anyone other than recruits. If it *does* have something to offer, that offering should not be under the control of those who regard any discussion of the discipline with outsiders as "watering down" or "popularization."

Clearly, teachers have failed if they do not offer knowledge in a form their students can assimilate and find meaningful. Although academic culture sometimes regards the development of students as less challenging than the development of a field, effective teaching calls not only for a synthesis of material that specialists may never bother to make, but a sensitivity to various kinds of people that is more common in a clinician, say, than in a behavioral researcher or a scholar. So valuable a combination of skills should hardly be accorded a lower status in our academic system than even run-of-the-mill research work.

In academic life, a bargain is struck by which we gain a standard to meet, an identity to adopt, and colleagues to quarrel with, but we may suffer a degree of isolation within the structure thus created. Undergraduate teaching must be directed beyond the field. We must either treat students as if they were all protospecialists, or widen the programs for preparing teachers so they learn to organize their thoughts around questions students actually have. PhD programs can accommodate the latter alternative much more fully by including the teaching practicum and encouraging intellectual work directed at the challenges of the classroom as well as at the referees of scholarly journals.

# 6

# Campus
# Programs
# on
# Teaching

Most campuses suffer from an anemic pedagogical culture. New institutionwide programs for teaching would
counteract the present undernourishment. Campus
teaching institutes may be one remedy. If they are carefully planned, such teaching centers can produce a number of benefits of long-range significance both to participants and institutions.

IN THEORY, PROFESSORS COULD INDIVIDUALLY ARRANGE FOR students, friends, widely admired teachers, or consultants on pedagogy to evaluate their work in detail and discuss their reactions. Some of this is already happening, but not to any great extent. In theory, too, groups of professors and students could simply get together in order to share and deepen their knowledge about learning as an activity. Some of this happens too, but few structures exist to intensify and draw others into these conversations. Departments could, and some do, offer training to their own graduate students about the very demanding job of being a college teacher, apart from the disciplinary knowledge that must be mastered. But even where an effort is made, we know of few departments in which programs on pedagogy call forth the same intensity and sophistication as ordinary course work. As a result, few institutions benefit from a rich pedagogical culture that would support the improvement of teaching.

If the pedagogical culture is generally undernourished, the problem is not a lack of ideas or even of people who acknowledge, to some degree, a need to make use of these ideas. But what is the individual college teacher to do? Imagine a professor who got to the office one morning and decided, for whatever reason, to make a deliberate effort to improve the quality and range of his or her own teaching. Exactly how, on a given campus, would that professor obtain the necessary information, practice, and pedagogical colleagueship? If facilities are available, to what extent must a professor define himself or herself as being in need of help in order to take part? Whatever its name, is the program regarded as remedial or ritualistic, rather than developmental? And why would a professor suddenly decide to make a special effort in the company of others?

In general, the task of learning how to teach has been left to individual graduate students, and the task of learning how to improve teaching, to individual professors. Programs to support this work, where they exist at all, are usually lodged within departments, as in the seminar for teaching assistants in freshman English. Nearly all departmental programs on teaching, however, suffer severe limitations. They tend to focus on large introductory courses, which, under current conditions, are often the least attractive forms of teaching. They depend on faculty who themselves lack a system of supports for their work as teachers and who often are bored by it and subtly devalue it. They seldom have access either to experts from outside the department or to facilities such as videotape and other equipment. And even if they do, students work only with those in their discipline, although there is much greater advantage in working with strangers with whom they do not have to compete— strangers who often share the innocence of undergraduates about their discipline.

---

Imagine a professor who got to the office
one morning and decided to make a deliberate effort
to improve the quality and range of his or her own teaching.
Exactly how, on a given campus,
would that professor obtain the necessary information,
practice, and pedagogical colleagueship?
If facilities are available, to what extent
must a professor define himself or herself as
being in need of help in order to take part?
Whatever its name, is the program
regarded as remedial or ritualistic, rather than
developmental? And why would a professor suddenly decide
to make a special effort in the company of others?

---

If only for these reasons, a program for teaching deserves to be sponsored by the institution as a whole. Without it, graduate students in some departments would not have access to any program, and even if each department on campus could somehow be persuaded to put together a program for its own students, support for that program would almost inevitably take second place to disciplinary concerns. In contrast, a campuswide program could be devoted solely to training in pedagogy. It could provide contact across disciplinary lines, a critical mass of participants, a sufficient range of teaching styles and assumptions. And it could enlist the services of specialists. Through the program, people would share a running commentary on what they were doing as teachers and as learners, a self-reflective commentary that would serve the purpose of faculty development. A program so far-reaching requires coordination, certain facilities, and a number of staff people in addition to the faculty associates: in short, a campus teaching center or institute.

But a campus teaching institute that tried to do the whole job itself would inevitably fail, although it might help a small number of graduate students and faculty. A successful institute would serve mainly to organize a process of observation and reflection about teaching among professors, graduate students, undergraduates, the staff of the institute, and in some cases visitors and consultants. It would differ both from the model of the resource center that simply makes facilities available to whomever happens to come in, and from the model of the training center that singlehandedly assumes responsibility for the quality of teaching. For the needs sketched here, the first model would be too weak and the second, presumptuous. Instead, the campus teaching institute would organize the energies of both faculty and graduate students to create a program in which they, rather than an institute staff, were the key participants.

---

**New experiences are essential to faculty
development. Faculty who have forgotten what it is to face
new challenges have lost touch with the situation
in which their students normally exist.
For this reason, sustaining the
sensibility of a learner is probably more valuable
to a teacher than any set of tips or techniques.**

---

The establishment of an institute would require strong leadership from presidents, deans, and respected faculty members. Although an institute would not cost much money, it would cost something. And in a time of retrenchment, this means shaving funds off some parts of an existing budget. Although an institute would not interfere with departmental prerogatives, it would absorb some energy from people who, in most cases, belong to departments. And although the staff for an institute would in some cases be found on campus, in other cases the best people for the job would be found outside. So without the active, consistent support of academic officials at the highest level, the idea of an institute would not likely be put into practice. Apart from their role in the recruitment and promotion of faculty, these officials could make their largest contribution to the quality of teaching through supporting programs for faculty development.

Faculty are accustomed to starting new programs within a department, to having nonacademic programs such as those for student services set up outside the department, and even to working in research centers with people from other disciplines. But for most, the challenge of taking part in a teaching institute outside the department would be new. The unfamiliar often arouses resistance, which is commonly attributed to other causes. Yet new experiences are essential to faculty development. Faculty who have forgotten what it is to face new challenges have lost touch with the situation in which their students normally exist. For this reason, sustaining the sensibility of a learner is probably more valuable to a teacher than any set of tips or techniques.

Faculty could take part in the work of the campus teaching institute in several ways. They could serve as visitors in a widespread program of observing in the classroom. They would go at a teacher's request to visit his or her classes, which they could subsequently discuss. If the teacher had asked that the class be unobtrusively taped, they could review portions on tape, noting points of interaction, and examining assumptions on which it was based. Not many professors have yet had the experience of watching their own work on a video recorder, which, far from being "just another gadget," offers a unique and graphic basis for self-reflection on teaching performance. Apart from colleagues, a professor could ask the class itself to review his or her work, or he could simply use the

---

**Undergraduates might serve as subjects
in a study conducted by members of the faculty,
but some would also be asked to
observe a variety of classes and educational settings,
and then discuss them with other observers.
As students learn to judge their teachers more skillfully, they
will appreciate more fully the extent to which
good teaching depends on their own responses.**

---

videotape facility to play back the performance in private.

A professor who showed a special talent as an observer and critic of teaching could become a faculty associate of the institute, devoting a fraction of his or her teaching schedule to its activities, and receive official credit for this as a form of teaching. Clearly, this form of association would have to be worked out with the various departments, but the institution could support it by providing that a department contributing more than its share of faculty time would not suffer in relation to other departments.

Finally, a professor could take part in the work of the institute through special projects, such as a study of students or faculty. Psychologists, sociologists, and members of other disciplines have conducted research on students for a number of decades, but reading their research reports is no substitute for direct involvement, in part because undergraduates today differ remarkably from their predecessors. Without any of the participants devoting an inordinate amount of time to the project, such a study would be valuable not only in what the faculty discovered, but in the knowledge among students that they were being listened to. The subjects of inquiry could range from reactions to a particular course to styles of learning or the effects of student culture on formal education.

Like faculty, undergraduates would participate in the work of the institute in a number of ways. As noted above, some might serve as subjects in a study conducted by members of the faculty, but some would also be asked to observe closely a variety of classes and educational settings, and then discuss them with other observers, with the teacher, and with one another. As students learn to judge their teachers more skillfully, they will appreciate more fully the extent to which good teaching depends on their own responses.

As for graduate students and assistant professors, the institute could not only render private and confidential service for the sake of improving teaching but could also certify teaching performance for the record—provided that the two functions are kept sharply separate. Upon request, the institute could arrange for a team of observers, perhaps from another institution, to visit a young teacher's classes, describe his or her methods and areas of mastery and certify whatever degree of teaching effectiveness they find. So far, whenever critics of higher education have urged that teaching be given more weight in personnel choices, the answer has come that dossiers bulge with data on the candidate's skill at paper writing and exam taking but say little about his or her teaching. A graduate student should be able to submit reports by trained evaluators who have observed the student teaching on a number of occasions in a variety of settings. Each student should have work evaluated by several visitors to avoid bias against a certain personality or approach, though any evaluation intended for a third party should be made only at the request of the student. A campus teaching institute could arrange for official observers to compile evaluations of various teaching episodes, and the missing evidence would at last come into currency.

In the absence of data other than rumors about teaching skills, proponents of good teaching are unable to make a strong case for their candidates, and until such evidence comes into being, professors so inclined will be able to claim that a good research man is probably competent as a teacher—at least until this assumption is flagrantly disproved—or that since teaching is so hard to assess reliably, it should be given little weight in hiring and promotion.

Evidence of teaching ability can of course be collected at any age, and people who are slow to establish their competence should have repeated opportunities to do so. Nevertheless, evaluation should start with people now in graduate school and follow them into their initial periods of employment. It should also begin with assistant professors and follow them into their period of tenure.

Campus teaching institutes would generate their own demand, for universities that went to the trouble of training their graduate students would want to hire young faculty with similar training, and that desire would produce a log-rolling effect. If a number of prestigious schools adopted the plan, others would have to follow suit lest their graduates suffer in the competition for jobs. By generating dossiers on teaching competence, leading graduate schools would cater to a demand that already exists but now has very little data to go on.

The steps outlined above would create a market for good teachers, along with a system for helping teachers improve. A graduate student who had taken full advantage of a campus teaching institute and built up a record of certified performance would have, as it were, negotiable paper to add to his or her dossier in applying for a first job. So would the assistant professor seeking tenure or another job.

Thoughtful reformers have asked whether serious assessment of teaching would itself create new resentments, resistances, and distortions as this activity too is brought within the meritocratic sphere. For example, there is the danger of teachers playing to whomever is given the power to evaluate them, whether students, colleagues, or outsiders. But professors already play to very strong norms they perceive within the disciplines, and those norms affect their choice of subjects, their modes of analysis, and their styles of writing. Further, the availability of funding has not been entirely without influence on the choice of research topics. Complaining that to invite observation of teaching is to subject the teacher to subtle restrictions is merely saying that teaching would thus share the fate of the more professional aspects of the academic life. This, to be sure, is not an unmixed blessing. The pressures of having performances judged would be alleviated, however, by opportunities to obtain a variety of reactions, usually from people one respects. Evaluations for the record would require much less time than, and would be kept strictly separate from, the major work of the institute including teachers' informal visits to one another's classes and confidential discussions of them.

Clearly, if a campus teaching institute succeeded in its various missions even to a modest degree, it would repay the effort re-

---

Campus teaching institutes would generate
their own demand, for universities that went to the trouble
of training their graduate students would want
to hire young faculty with similar training,
and that desire would produce a log-rolling effect.
If a number of prestigious schools adopted the plan,
others would have to follow suit lest their
graduates suffer in the competition for jobs. By
generating dossiers on teaching competence,
leading graduate schools would cater to a demand that
already exists but now has very little data to go on.

---

quired, both in terms of the quality of education on that campus and in terms of the competitive edge it would give to its graduate students. The cost in dollars would not be large, nor would the program require complex facilities. Videotape units would be helpful but not absolutely necessary: a simple audio recorder can preserve much of the flavor of a class. Apart from the cost of a small staff, composed at least in part of faculty on release time, the institute would rely mainly on the energy of those professors who benefit from it. And an institution should give official recognition to work for faculty development if only because the alternative is a wasteful repetition, sometimes over decades, of teaching performances that fall short of the faculty's potential.

The work of the institute would grow out of teaching actually being done on the campus, and in turn would affect the shape of the curriculum as well as pedagogical styles. Courses and programs developed through the institute could help integrate a curriculum otherwise compartmentalized by disciplines. Its function would be irreplaceable. Properly introduced, organized, and supported, it would prepare graduate students to teach, create a market in teaching skills, draw professors into a broad and practical consideration of pedagogy, encourage the serious and imaginative participation of students, make use of expertise about student development and teaching techniques, and devise courses and programs unlikely to emerge without it.

# 7

# The
# Role
# of
# Experts

Pedagogic development through teaching institutes may be further enhanced by teaching consultants from the outside, used in a suitable mix with the campus faculty. Expertise in this area should be utilized wherever it is available.

IN ESTABLISHING A CAMPUS TEACHING INSTITUTE, THE WORK of outside experts would not always be necessary. Even at their worst professors at least have direct experience in teaching. If some of the more reflective and resourceful among them take a hand in creating an institute, others would soon profit through associating with them in an active program. Given persistent leadership, members of any faculty can go a long way in helping themselves by drawing on their varied experience in teaching, raising questions about particular cases, observing the process of education more closely as a result, trying new methods, and helping one another evaluate the outcomes.

Nevertheless, professors are not generally accustomed to collaborating intensely and systematically in this kind of work. Some of them are reticent about discussing their experience as teachers, and many do not yet know how to discuss the process of teaching and learning as richly or precisely as they could if they received the kind of training and support described above.

In this situation, an administrator may seek special help in establishing a lively campus program on teaching. He may arrange for consultants to talk with a sample of faculty and observe their work, discuss the preliminary findings, share knowledge about the process of learning and student development, help colleagues learn to evaluate one another's work—in short, perform some of the services that a campus teaching institute would regularly perform. In doing so, an administrator would honor the adage that the best way to start a program is not to propose a structure but to get people involved in whatever it will do once it is formally established. Whatever the need for "self-study," for recommendations on the eventual shape of a program on teaching, there is no reason for a delay in providing services to teachers interested in taking advantage of them.

Outside experts have several advantages over members of the faculty in providing initial services. Unlike many professors, they are not necessarily identified with a particular faction on campus, a political viewpoint, or an ideology about education. While professors may recognize that certain of their colleagues undoubtedly have more expertise than others in teaching, they might accept help more gracefully from an outsider who, besides, has the benefit of experience at a wider range of institutions. Nor can faculty members afford to give a new program the energy that an outside expert, engaged for this specific purpose, can bring to it. A teaching institute would always require a first-rate person to coordinate its activities,

---

An administrator may seek special help
in establishing a lively campus program on teaching.
He may arrange for consultants to talk
with a sample of faculty and observe their work,
discuss the preliminary findings, share
knowledge about the process of learning and student
development, help colleagues learn to evaluate one
another's work—in short, perform some
of the services that a campus teaching institute
would regularly perform. In doing so,
an administrator would honor the adage
that the best way to start a program is not
to propose a structure but to get people
involved in whatever it will do
once it is formally established.
Whatever the need for "self-study,"
for recommendations on the eventual shape of a program
on teaching, there is no reason for a delay
in providing services to teachers
interested in taking advantage of them.

---

and he or she might also have a staff; but the work of the institute would depend heavily on the expertise developed by members of the faculty who would participate as observers of teaching, discussants, and in some cases more fully as associates.

Just as there are not enough faculty well trained as teachers, so there are not as many consultants as are needed to assist in the necessary training and pedagogical support of teachers. Ordinarily one might reach the conclusion that not much can be done until somebody trains a corps of consultants, but that, in turn, will not happen until a forceful demand for their services develops. This is a formula for infinite delay. What is needed are a number of programs for pedagogical consulting, in which training will occur mainly through actual consultation work at colleges, led and supervised by the experienced people already available. Such a program would be immediately useful to colleges and would help to meet the demand it would generate for these specialists.

Consultants would help to get programs started; a small staff of resident experts would coordinate the teaching institutes, offer special services, and help to train the faculty; administrators charged with improving the quality of teaching would provide the necessary leadership and support for the program; and certain faculty members would, as associates of the institute, extend the work done by its resident staff.

A word of warning. There have been few programs for faculty development of the kind we outline here. As administrators and faculty themselves take an interest in starting programs on teaching, consultants will offer to help and in some cases will present old services under the new label of "faculty development." One test of their quality is whether the consultant is prepared to move quickly into actual work with faculty. People can discuss what needs to be done forever, can study their own situation to the point of boredom and exhaustion, with or without the help of consultants. To be sure, "further study is necessary": it always is. But nothing more needs to be known for work with faculty to begin. The unique contribution an outside expert can make is to bring teachers together to discuss, not teaching in the abstract, but their own experiences.

# 8

# Evaluation
# for
# What?

The great game of grading offers relief from the ambiguities of learning, but the two should not be confused. Good learning presumes a vulnerability, which grading as a sorting-out process often prevents. A separation of the two is possible, with third-party assessment of both students and teachers performed in an atmosphere of confidentiality.

REFORMERS OF HIGHER EDUCATION HAVE OFTEN PROCEEDED by subtraction, claiming virtue according to how many elements of the traditional system they could do without. Thus, an experimental program might praise itself because it had no required courses, no lectures—and certainly no grades.

In particular, many an educational prospectus has cited grading as the chief source of pedagogical ills, a stimulant to competition and even fraudulence, a discouragement to risk taking, a system of self-fulfilling prophecy that teaches students their place, and a rich source of more obvious kinds of unfairness. The conclusion was obvious: away with grades.

Yet the force of these charges can drive toward a very different conclusion: that people should be judged on their work not less but much more fully, so long as the judgment is intended for the use of the students rather than registrars, admission deans, or potential employers. Clearly our society now expects higher education to certify its graduates. Assuming that colleges and universities ought to perform this function, the question remains of who should make the necessary judgments. Should a teacher be required to judge his or her own students for the benefit of third parties?

Unlike physicians and attorneys, college teachers do not hold their records in confidence but prepare them explicitly for the use of people outside the classroom. Students of course understand clearly that what passes between them and their teachers is more like testimony than privileged communication. One consequence is that students seek, in talking with teachers, to build a record or to make a case, rather than to expose their ignorance, failings, and confusion or to try something they are unsure of.

The main purpose of grading is not to help students learn but to place them, both within the academy and later in society. Sorting people out is generally a much easier task for faculty than educating them more fully, and for students, playing the great game of grades offers relief from the ambiguities of learning.

If grades were no worse than a dubious motive for learning or a misleading report of accomplishment, the topic would not warrant much space in an essay on faculty development. However, elliptical grading for the benefit of third parties may also strongly alter the process it is meant to motivate and assess. People frequently learn by admitting ignorance, trying various possibilities, and correcting errors. Such a process depends on vulnerability, and that cannot be sustained when the need to get a good grade induces students to pose as more knowledgeable than curious. Ideally, a teacher might offer a model of a person who does not need to know everything and can inquire in public; but students can afford to emulate such a model only if they will not be marked down for the awkwardness, mistakes, and false starts inherent in genuine exploration.

Similarly, a teacher is more likely to offer such a model when allied unequivocally with students than when required to act as both helper and certifier. If we separate the function of helping students from that of grading them for the benefit of third parties, teachers would escape a long-standing conflict in their roles, and students could give up their self-defensive attempts to feign mastery. Excused from having to certify the performance of their own students, teachers could serve them less ambiguously, setting high standards, evaluating work privately, diagnostically, and early. What a student could do at the end of a course or sequence would be judged by others in the university or perhaps by outsiders.

Of course, ineptitude or rigidity in outside examining might reduce the autonomy of teachers who can now make up their own exams, stressing what they hope to have taught. If someone else wrote the exam, that person would thereby indirectly control the content of the teaching to the extent that students would pressure their teacher to cover material corresponding to what might be on the exam.

The problem is not insurmountable, however, especially if exams are not created by a small number of national boards that reflect a single consensus and lock the subject into an orthodoxy of boundaries and style. Local arrangements and possibly a wide range of exams set by professional groups or regional examining universities are likely to be more flexible and satisfactory. For example, professors might write their own exams but have them graded by teachers not involved in the same courses; or they might explain the content of the course to colleagues who would then create the exam, a procedure that in itself might lead to fruitful exchanges and require a clear definition of goals. Perhaps a mixture of local and multi-institutional exams could best allow for meaningful comparisons and also for differences in the pedagogical objectives of individual professors and departments. Disciplinary associations could take a major role both in defining a range of competencies and in arranging for evaluations of students by competent judges other than their own teachers. In any case, exams should be limited neither to the idiosyncrasies of a single teacher nor to any single form negotiated by a distant national board. Except in the case of "objective" questions, grading should be based on the judgment of more than one reader, with arrangements for due process in the case of appeals.

Under the present system, most students cram for exams anyway. Why not let them pursue their education most of the time, in alliance with their teachers, and then shape their knowledge for an outside exam in the last week or two? Motivation would still be linked in part to grades, but the students could afford to reveal themselves, take chances, and inquire more freely than is now the case. The course would have to be inherently more appealing. And if the teacher were perceived as a helper rather than a grader, charges of authoritarianism would probably decrease, even if he or she firmly asserted expertise and standards. The system of detached evaluation would cost no more than the present method: a teacher would simply evaluate somebody else's students while his own were evaluated by a colleague. Detaching course work from certification would have special benefits for the student who now takes certain courses simply because they are required, not because he wants to extend his curiosity, take some risks, or master the subject for a well-defined purpose. A system of credit by external exam, if the criteria were clearly defined in advance, would free a lot of energy for intrinsically motivated learning and thus make students more interesting to their teachers as well.

Whatever exam system serves as the basis for grading and certification, students still need evaluation of their work as they go along. Teachers have always been free to offer such evaluation to students, apart from the formalities of grading. Whether in the form of marginal comments on papers or discussion in the office or classroom, evaluations have a considerable impact. Students need to know what they are capable of, where their thought has led, what they need to work on, and where they can go next. Every good teacher deals with these questions to some degree, often primarily in the course of assigning grades. Nonetheless, the system of grading works against the process of diagnostic and supportive evaluation, because students have a strong incentive to conceal any weakness or doubt they feel. In this sense, the main disadvantage of grading one's own students is not the risk of unfairness or incompleteness but the effect of the practice on the relationship between teacher and student. By now this relationship is so pervasively supported by the school system as well as by the colleges that a change from grading by the teacher to a system of external exams will not automatically lead students to deal with teachers as unequivocal helpers instead of part-time judges. To create this new relationship will itself require the breaking of bad habits so far reinforced by the educational system.

Unfortunately, some critics of teaching now propose applying to its practitioners a system of grading no more sophisticated than the one teachers have long applied to students—at the price of further warping the relationship between them. In response to complaints about lackluster teaching, observers have proposed that teaching be evaluated and assessed, and that the better teachers be rewarded, the worse given a warning and possibly some help. Under such a system, a teacher might perish even if he publishes, unless he also is said to have taught reasonably well.

Advocates of student evaluations argue that students are the only people who observe the whole course; that the quality of the course is meaningless except insofar as it reaches them; and that if students write inadequate or insensitive evaluations, they can be taught, as a useful part of their education, to write better ones. Some institutions have developed elaborate questionnaires for use in evaluating courses. Proponents claim, if only to soften the faculty's resistance, that the intention is not punitive but ameliorative; once a weakness is diagnosed, the teacher can learn how to improve.

Dissatisfaction with the performance of faculty, coupled with the growing number of underemployed PhDs, may allow boards and administrations to impose new controls, or at least try certain incentives. For example, the demand for accountability may lead to a new apparatus for measuring the cost-effectiveness of teaching. However grotesque this ambition may seem to many teachers, it appeals to some legislators, board members, and administrators who doubt that students are getting their money's worth and who think that most educational budgets contain subsidies for the nonteaching ac-

---

Faculty development depends heavily
on the way faculty evaluate students, students
evaluate faculty, and colleagues evaluate one another.
As long as evaluations are made
primarily for the record rather than for the direct benefit of
the student or professor, those who teach
and those who learn will maintain
strong defenses against being found out.
Forced to frustrate or elude the kind
of evaluation that could help them, people
come to need it more as they can risk it less.
If institutions provided for evaluation
detached from career consequences, alongside
a system of certification by people other than a student's
own teachers, students and faculty alike would
have much more free space in which to develop.

---

tivities of professors. Whatever its possible value, however, no assessment system provides what is really necessary: namely, the means by which teachers can improve their work and the structural reforms necessary to sustain good teaching.

Along with students, teachers also need more assessment, not less, but they need it within a confidential relationship. Like students, teachers need opportunities to play from uncertainty as well as tested strength, to try new things, and to stumble: otherwise they are like people trying to learn a foreign language without making any mistakes. Any teacher should be able to get advice about teaching, try out new techniques, monitor his or her own performance, receive informed and confidential criticism, observe the work of other teachers, and discuss common problems—all without prejudice to administrative decisions about tenure or salary.

A developmental approach to education calls for a new kind of detachment: for students the detachment of the process of learning from the certification of competence; and for teachers, detachment of efforts to improve teaching from official assessments of performance. Institutions should arrange to provide both students and teachers with much more diagnostic evaluation that will not be computed into the record made available to officials guarding the next set of gates.

People often speak of grades as tools to encourage students to work. In the absence of other motivations, however, of how much use is this one in stimulating the kind of learning that good teachers must hope will occur? If other motivations are brought into play, judgments recorded by teachers for the benefit of a third party become superfluous. The system of grading does give the faculty an obvious leverage over their students—at the cost, in large courses, of tedious work—but this kind of leverage may trap them within a sense of authority far less satisfying than the authority derived from their ability to help students deepen their interests, develop skills, and master a field.

This is not to say that student satisfaction must derive solely from the immediate joys of learning. Often learning is difficult, gratification deferred and uncertain. But in spite of widespread suspicions about the value of growing up, most students have some larger purpose in mind—a career, a set of interests, a cause, a desire for intellectual mastery. If not, the immaturity and shallowness of their motivations ought to be revealed to them as early as possible; they should not be perpetuated by either the students' thoughtless acceptance or flat rejection of the evaluative system. To the extent that an academic system has relied for its motivation on the threat of bad grades, an escape from this threat may lead to rebellion against or neglect of academic obligations. Yet this very reaction would argue for a sustained, intense effort to develop new incentives, not for a return to such dubious controls.

Faculty development depends heavily on the way faculty evaluate students, students evaluate faculty, and colleagues evaluate one another. As long as evaluations are made primarily for the record rather than for the direct benefit of the student or professor, those who teach and those who learn will maintain strong defenses against being found out. Forced to frustrate or elude the kind of evaluation that could help them, people come to need it more as they can risk it less. If institutions provided for evaluation detached from career consequences, alongside a system of certification by people other than a student's own teachers, students and faculty alike would have much more free space in which to develop.

# 9

# Grants
# for
# Teaching

National resources for enhancing pedagogical competence are woefully lacking, and grants should be provided similar to those given for research. The dual hierarchy
of quality teaching and intellectual work and research
needs to be legitimated, with grant dollars attached to
both.

DESPITE ADMINISTRATIVE CONTROLS AND SPORADIC PRES-
sure from students, it is the faculty who determine what will be
taught, establish certain styles of teaching, and set the terms, as it
were, of their educational contract with students. Many observers
believe that the more faculty who are required to frame or even simply to approve a program, the less chance it has of ever being established. When acting as a whole, or through the often intricate committee structure supposedly representative of the whole, faculty can
display remarkable ingenuity in frustrating one another and their
students as well.

According to the common wisdom, a program that does not carry
credit or is clearly extracurricular stands a better chance of being
approved than a revision of the basic curriculum. The faculty finds
it comparatively easy to accept "experiments" and ad hoc additions
that isolate serious reforms on the periphery. Individual faculty
members often have considerable latitude for what they do in their
own established courses, but in many cases proposals to substitute
a new course must run a fierce gauntlet.

Aware of these impediments and often bruised by them, some reformers have wearily concluded that the best strategy for change in
higher education is either to start a new institution or to find agencies outside the colleges and universities that will directly support
individual professors. One model for this is the present system of research grants, which bypasses the institution and deals directly
with individual scholars and investigators.

Let us imagine for a moment that the real business of colleges and
universities, the basic job of their professors, were research. Nonetheless, the young would require education, even if they did not always demand it; faculty would therefore be expected, in their spare
hours as it were, to offer courses. In such a world, it would soon become apparent that pedagogy was a hard business. The young have
diverse needs they cannot always clearly define or even know. The
culture keeps changing, as do the specialized fields to which the professors are primarily devoted. True, faculty with a special love for

the challenge of teaching could do a lot on their own, but many of them would finally reach a point where help was necessary. They would draw up lists of special facilities they needed, periods for preparation, arrangements for field work, funds for collaborating with other teachers, "resource people," and the like. And then what? If an institution, having paid for the research of its faculty and supported the necessary labs and libraries, had no funds left over for pedagogical purposes, where could the faculty turn?

In this situation somebody might well hit upon the device of offering resources for pedagogy through a national competition open to all qualified professors who wanted to teach. Perhaps a set of competitions could be arranged according to fields or kind of reform. Professors would describe what it was they wanted to teach, review similar efforts described in the literature, state their goals, describe in detail their methods, name their collaborators, submit a budget, and so forth. Various panels would review the applications and choose among them. And no doubt people who could attract the kind of money this would bring would become more desirable to their institutions.

Still, this kind of grant would not necessarily lead to cooperation on campus, and it might lead to difficulties. Money that comes from politicians has always been a threat to the academic freedom of those who take unpopular stands. There would understandably be a demand for proof that the money had accomplished something, and to get such proof a whole new variety of tests would have to be written and administered. Because the problems of devising sensitive and fair measurements of teaching effectiveness are so great, those tests are not likely to be reliable. Nor would it increase the flexibility of an individual professor to require him or her to go through a long and complex application procedure and to deal with various reviewers and distant bureaucrats rather than simply share the resources of his own institution. Planning a curriculum that depended in part on decisions made elsewhere about the money that would be available would be exceedingly difficult.

Fortunately, agencies can develop a less troublesome and intrusive method of allocating special funds for pedagogy. They can give money not so much to individual faculty members as to institutions or groups that propose to establish teaching institutes and evaluation services or to groups of colleagues who work together in planning, teaching, and sharing their experience of various special programs. This kind of funding would encourage some people on each campus to collaborate on the improvement of teaching, instead of either giving up hope—which is now often the case—or competing with one another in a program of individual grants. Collaborative grants could go to campus teaching institutes, to colleague groups formed to offer courses, or to other programs outside the present structure. They probably should not go to departments unless they show a very strong commitment to a well-conceived plan for improving the quality or nature of their program. Otherwise, they could easily absorb pedagogical assets in support of what they have been doing all along by pasting new labels on traditional practices.

Pedagogical grants to institutions would differ from research grants in several ways. Since their goal would be the maximum development of students in a certain area, rather than the advancement of a discipline, the grants would be spread more broadly than research money has been. They would be given to those institutions with the best programs for helping the students they have, regardless of the presumed abilities of these students, their backgrounds, or their cognitive styles. If they were awarded on the basis of how much the institution would do for its students, colleges that now receive few awards for advanced research might nevertheless merit pedagogical grants. Such a program would have political appeal and also would extend the reach of pedagogical innovations to students most in need of them.

Since much of what is already published falls far below the best work in each field, there is no reason why everyone in academic life should have to honor the single standard of publication. The academic world should adequately recognize a dual hierarchy of value and support both teaching and research by appropriate funding and institutional arrangements. The best researchers could then continue their special work, and people who are primarily teachers could undertake the self-renewal, planning, and cooperation necessary to be very good at what they do.

Ideally, they could undertake this work together rather than in isolation. Pedagogical design calls for informed colleagueship, which does not always follow disciplinary lines. A campus teaching institute could introduce people who might help one another in this way and give them a setting for their work together. In some cases they might decide to offer various joint courses; in others, simply to confer regularly on courses that each would individually offer. Open discussions about pedagogy often occur more easily in a group drawn from a number of disciplines than within the formal structure of a single department. In planning a new kind of course, a professor often needs help not with the content but rather with the matter of how to deal with the content, how to lead students into it, and help them start working with it. Sometimes colleagues from other fields can, if only through their own questions and curiosity, help a teacher in ways that an expert in the field might not so easily do.

Small grants to teachers for special pedagogical efforts would be particularly helpful. At present, support for a course is often limited to a salary for the professor, perhaps a stipend for a teaching assistant, the use of a classroom and some office space, and access to the library and to machines for duplicating, showing pictures, and the like. But some pedagogical efforts require additional resources or a somewhat different allocation of money. And small grants could provide encouragement and elicit imaginative teaching from at least a substantial fraction of the faculty.

It is fair to conclude that a college or university is not making the best use of its pedagogical budget unless it reserves at least a small percentage to be given in the form of pedagogical grants to members of its faculty. The percentage could usefully rise well above the amounts in discretionary funds that deans sometimes have for similar purposes. Ideally, the awarding of pedagogical grants would be coordinated with the work of the campus teaching institute. In any case, the program should be administered by an official or a panel in a position to make judgments on the merits of each proposal, without regard to departmental quotas. Reserving and attracting funds for this purpose, as for the establishment of teaching institutes, should command top priority for any official charged with the quality of education.

# 10

## Intellectual Mobility

It is harder to improve an existing job than to move to a new one, but diminished faculty mobility may provide opportunities for in-place enhancing of professional competence. Multiple professional identifications, rather than identification only with one's own discipline, is a break with academic traditions that would provide networks of interests and intellectual integration.

F ACULTY DEVELOPMENT OFFERS A SET OF NEW RELATION-
ships. If professors were no longer in the double-bind of having both
to educate and to certify their own students, the relationship between them would undoubtedly change. If colleagues had structures
through which to evaluate teaching and to share knowledge about
learning, they could broaden their helpfulness to one another. And
if, instead of being largely monopolized by departments, professors
could join one another more flexibly for the purposes of teaching as
well as research, they might create new relationships that would
benefit both faculty and students.

Institutions can turn the current tight job market to their advantage by enlarging the traditional definition of mobility. They can give
their faculty chances not only to move from one job or rank to
another but also to develop their intellectual mastery beyond patterns now created by rigid departmental monopolies. Mobility in the
old sense no doubt offers satisfaction to misplaced or underappreci-
ated people, but it does little to widen the scope of jobs within the
system. Of course, it is harder to improve a given job than to accept
a new one. But diminished mobility among institutions may allow us
to redirect a degree of academic energy to the serious question of
how to enlarge existing jobs and to develop the skills and self-awareness of the people who hold them.

Many believe that institutions can significantly improve teaching
simply by giving it more weight in hiring and promotion, by reducing
class size, or by assuring more contact between faculty and students. However, good teaching depends both on practical training in
the necessary skills and on other kinds of work a professor is doing.
Academic dogma urges that teaching depends on research and that
no one can stay fresh in the classroom without keeping up with what
is going on and, if possible, contributing to it. But given the present
criteria for promotion, it is no accident that certain kinds of work

are done and other kinds neglected or even scorned; and the latter group includes much that would substantially benefit students, society, and faculty whose interests do not always stay within departmental boundaries.

Any way of dividing up knowledge will dissatisfy some people. Rather than have departments, some colleges, like general education programs of the past, organize knowledge simply into the three familiar areas: humanities, social sciences, and natural sciences. Such an arrangement at least has the virtue of making fewer boundaries. Subdivisions may focus on geographic regions (East Asia, for example), "excluded" groups (women, blacks), philosophic approaches (phenomenology), developmental stages (adolescence), social or human problems (urban studies, population control, ecology). The list can easily be extended.

Like the departmental structure, however, these arrangements often identify teachers primarily or solely with a single academic

---

Academic dogma urges that teaching depends
on research and that no one can stay fresh
in the classroom without keeping up
with what is going on and, if
possible, contributing to it. It is no accident
that certain kinds of work are done
and other kinds neglected or even scorned;
and the latter group includes much that
would substantially benefit students, society, and
faculty whose interests do not always
stay within departmental boundaries.

---

unit, whether department, division, interest group, or institute. The assumption that a professor ought to belong to a single unit reflects a metaphor about knowledge that governs much of academic life. Knowledge is imagined as if it were a geographic region divided into "areas." Each man has his "field," which adjoins a number of others: he must "cover the ground" in his teaching and "push back the frontier," if possible, in his research. While pushing out, however, he must take care not to "trespass" into a neighboring field. As among departments, so among the many smaller parcels within them, "good fences make good neighbors." Occasionally, and only on the frontier, a fence gets rearranged and a new field is created, but seldom are professors licensed and encouraged to cross fences or create enterprises that involve a number of fields. Only undergraduates, swooping about in the college curriculum, are expected to see the whole, at least until they are "brought down to earth" and made to "dig deeply" into a single field. Although the proprietors of most of these fields put in some cash crops in order to stay solvent, they prefer to grow mainly for home consumption.

The argument for the departmental monopoly of the curriculum and of most professors' allegiance rests upon a network of assumptions: that each professor belongs within the turf of a single academic unit and shouldn't "spread himself too thin"; that no academic unit should be created unless it is designed to last forever; that once trained in a field a professor ought to stay there and not "wander" like a nomad; that a person should be allowed to teach or do research only if he has obtained a degree in the same discipline; and that an academic unit can operate successfully only if linked both to the journals and the hiring market of a permanent national association.

None of these assumptions is frivolous. The present academic structure evolved to meet a variety of needs and to provide important defenses for its members. Proposals for alternative or even supplementary structures call into question a pattern of departmental commitments which, however severe their limitations, at least provide a sure professional home. Like most other people, professors need identity and job security, and like most institutions colleges require competence and a measure of stability. The rise of the disciplines has produced a somewhat rigid structure but it has also fostered impressive skills.

Nonetheless, there are other ways to picture knowledge, and an unexamined metaphor is not worth teaching by. In making national reputations and sharing academic culture, professors have become more cosmopolitan, but in terms of the way intellectual energies are distributed, many academics have become more "local," more confined to narrow perspectives. As an aggregate, the university has become more complex and multifarious, but the impression of breadth and flexibility fades when we shift the focus from the institution as a whole to a given member of it. For most professors a specialty is less like a variegated city than like a small town.

Academic structure could assist faculty development much more than it now does. A discipline can be seen as a particular set of questions, methods, and types of knowledge—some of which other fields share. The elements could be rearranged in many ways. Some scholars have proposed that institutions allow groups of faculty to get together, create new disciplines, and even offer degrees, thus adding to the current roster of departments. This is a valuable idea because it offers a mechanism for rearrangements and for new intellectual enterprises, but it continues to assume that a professor will identify with no more than a single academic unit.

What could a university look like if we moved away from this assumption? What if every professor were given an opportunity for multiple identifications? To some extent this already occurs, through institutes, special programs, and so forth. But what if this were the norm? Beginnings have been made at some institutions with cluster colleges, where a professor can belong both to a department and to a college, which itself may have a special bent. At other places a university may offer a half-time appointment in one department and half-time in another or at an institute. Although some institutes are departmental creations, others deal with questions that obviously require the application of more than one discipline or that call for entirely new modes of knowledge. In general, however, most of these arrangements are supplements to a basic identification with a standard discipline.

If only to throw the present system into relief, imagine a faculty organized solely around colleague groups based on shared interests in certain puzzlements, social problems, methodologies, areas of the world, or philosophical approaches. A faculty member would ordinarily belong to more than one of these colleague groups. The groups would offer courses, including collaborative courses by two or more members. In an institution organized this way, some groups might last longer than others. Members of these groups might create national links with their colleagues in similar groups at other institutions, just as scholars do within the existing disciplines. Some colleague groups might be fairly conventional, others more adventurous or experimental. Some would preserve various disciplinary traditions; others might focus on questions or types of experience that the disciplines neglect.

---

**In making national reputations
and sharing academic culture, professors have
become more cosmopolitan, but
in terms of the way intellectual
energies are distributed, many academics have become
more "local," more confined to narrow perspectives.
As an aggregate, the university
has become more complex and multifarious, but
the impression of breadth and flexibility fades
when we shift the focus from
the institution as a whole to a given member
of it. For most professors a specialty
is less like a variegated city than like a small town.**

---

Originally a professor would be hired to serve in one or more groups for whose work he had already been trained, but within limits he could rearrange his set of interests by joining a new group and at some point leaving one of his original groups. The requirement for joining a new group would be, not certified competence in the field, but lively curiosity about it and a commitment to work within it. Such a structure would offer faculty an appropriate way of expanding their competence without, as it were, going back to graduate school, and in doing so these professors would set students an example of being open to the strange or risky instead of always playing from strength.

Such a utopia raises many obvious questions: how would faculty be hired, assessed, and promoted? How many professors really *want* to work closely with colleagues on their deepest intellectual interests? The current pattern suggests that every professor needs a little piece of knowledge to call his own, and the scarcity of collaborative courses suggests that few professors want to work with others. Academics face the dilemma that the only people they can *really* talk with are also the only ones with an indisputable right to criticize their work or, much worse, to ignore it. Still, the present system causes very considerable anxiety, and without structures that encourage collaboration we will never know whether that anxiety is necessary or whether, even if unavoidable, it might be put to better use.

Critics might wonder what would prevent these colleague groups from throwing rigor out the window or even catering to student fads: some enthusiasm is shallow or misguided, some thinking sloppy and pointless. But a group of colleagues associated around a special concern would not necessarily suffer these faults to a greater degree than departments or individual professors do now. A structure based on colleague groups would offer its members a shared task, comparative perspectives, and relatively open communication among specialists who now lack a meeting place.

Some people think that only departments keep the college from anarchy. Yet the present fragmentation of knowledge has itself produced a subtle form of anarchy because the isolation of each professor within his or her specialty reduces the communicative and ordering function that structures are supposed to perform. Far from encouraging anarchy, a system that allowed professors to belong to several groups would tie the faculty together in various networks of interests and provide the opportunity for various kinds of integration.

Some of the seemingly anti-intellectual trends among young people reflect in part their distaste for the way academic life is structured. The standard departmental courses do not engage the interest of many students and, even if they did, would not prepare them for their lives and work. What, then, should be done? Certainly we should neither turn the universities over to narrow vocational training, nor pander to transitory political or cultural fashions. A college or university should, however, be prepared to assist resourceful, imaginative, disciplined teachers in addressing problems of human life the curriculum now neglects. A system of colleague groups could provide a mechanism for doing so.

Within the prevailing academic structure, a professor identified with a single specialty and a single style can find mobility on campus only by building his or her own prestige, moving up in the department, and then attracting others to join it. To encourage faculty development, we ought to create space for intellectual as well as departmental mobility, for the average as well as the exceptionally brilliant professor. If arrangements were available through which faculty members could rekindle their interests, find new colleagues, explore new questions, and teach in new settings, then faculty might apply some of the immense energy now absorbed by academic gamesmanship to opportunities for their own development.

Of course, a faculty member trained by one department and then hired by another in his field and linked to the corresponding scholarly association may feel a touch of motion sickness when first exposed to the greater fluidity of multiple and shifting academic memberships. Such people may resist new arrangements because of an anxious commitment to a world they already know well, and resistance may prove intractable in places where power remains in the departments. But if the academic structure were seriously rearranged and multiple channels for development opened within it, faculty devotion to their local institutions would surely increase. Such internal career opportunities might also reduce the problem of "dead wood," now so frustrating not only to the departments involved but also to the professors who find no time to grow.

Although academic research is now done very largely within a disciplinary framework, in spite of efforts by some funding agencies to stimulate other kinds of work, the departments have not yet definitely absorbed the undergraduate curriculum. Exceptions keep intruding: general education, certain freshman seminars, special programs, experimental month-long courses tucked between two semesters of standard fare, courses given by institutes or interdepartmental committees. Within each of these structures, however, some of the work differs little from what departments already offer, and within the offerings of American higher education, such courses amount to a very small share.

---

**Some people think that only departments keep
the college from anarchy. Yet the present fragmentation
of knowledge has itself produced
a subtle form of anarchy because
the isolation of each professor within his or her specialty
reduces the communicative and ordering function
that structures are supposed to perform.
Far from encouraging anarchy, a system that
allowed professors to belong to several groups
would tie the faculty together in various networks
of interests and provide the opportunity
for various kinds of integration.
A structure based on colleague groups would
offer its members a shared task, comparative
perspectives, and relatively open communication
among specialists who now lack a meeting place.**

---

The point is *not* that departments are bad, but rather that no single method of dividing knowledge ought to enjoy a structural monopoly; *not* that disciplinary clusters are unnecessary, but that institutions should encourage other kinds of clusters as well; and finally, *not* that individual professors should be deprived of organization, but that most should be linked to a number of units rather than only one.

At a minimum, institutions could encourage faculty and student development by the creation of supplementary colleague groups authorized to give courses, even to supervise degree programs. For example, a member of a department could be allowed to divert a fraction, perhaps as much as half, of his or her time to work in a colleague group, which, like a department, would govern itself. Under this arrangement professors would not lose their departments but would gain colleague groups. When one colleague group reached the end of its usefulness, its members could join others, or take a hand in starting new ones.

The main difficulty here arises in the case of teachers early in their careers who do not yet have tenure but have hopes of getting it. So long as tenure is recommended solely by departments, young people will be reluctant to give less than full attention and allegiance to the potential sources of their security. Institutions could relieve this pressure by providing that departments are responsible for the quality of their contributions to colleague groups, or they could put control of tenure decisions in the hands of the units within which the candidate has taught, including the colleague groups.

The plan for a collateral system of colleague groups offers a form of intellectual mobility linked to the learning of students. Professors have always been able to work closely with a number of exceptional students who ranged beyond departmental fences, and to associate with friends from other fields, but they have seldom been able to band together with faculty and students from a variety of fields who share common interests and who wish to pursue them jointly, seriously, and within the structure of credits, degrees, facilities, and jobs normally supplied by the institution.

# 11

## Mid-Career Transitions

Providing insurance mechanisms to allow mid-career transitions into nonacademic work could make a very large difference to academic institutions in the late twentieth century. Intercampus faculty exchanges and provisions for mixing academic with nonacademic employment would also enhance academic performance in a period of contraction.

WITH THE HELP OF PROGRAMS SUCH AS THOSE OUTLINED IN preceding sections, colleges and universities could do much more than they generally have to help faculty develop in the course of their work on campus. Some faculty, however, would continue to grow bored with teaching or would remain trapped within the narrow frame of competence that had earlier brought them rewards. Other professors might find that the program itself reawakened ambitions outside academic life. Such people would benefit from a mid-career transition, and in the case of uninspired, resentful, or severely limited teachers, the institution clearly would benefit as well.

Yet very few professors, once given tenure, leave academic life until they retire. The tenure system provides an extraordinary incentive to faculty to stay on the job; it also fosters the myth that all will remain dedicated and effective as teachers for the next thirty years, and none will ever want to go into another line of work. Whatever happens to the tenure system, institutions could counterbalance the incentive to permanence with a program of insurance for mid-career changes. If a faculty member decided, in mid-career, to leave academic life for another vocation, the insurance plan would provide basic support during a few years of retraining or of becoming established in a new field. Along with the insurance benefits, faculty should have access to effective and discreet career counseling services.

Just as TIAA-CREF offer retirement plans to staff at all academic institutions, so an insurance plan for mid-career transitions could be organized to serve all colleges and universities. The plan could offer a rising rate of benefits up to an age after which few people would imagine shifting to a new kind of work and after which the benefits would simply offer a temptation to unusually early retirement. The cost of supporting a person for a few transitional years at the age of 45, say, is very small compared to the difference, over the next twenty years, between his or her salary and the salary of a replacement hired at the age of 25. Support for the transitional years might be pegged above the level of what a professor not being encouraged to stay would otherwise be receiving in salary, but under what a very attractive colleague of the same age was earning.

---

**Very few professors, once given tenure,
leave academic life until they retire.
The tenure system provides an extraordinary
incentive to faculty to stay on the job;
it also fosters the myth that all will
remain dedicated and effective as teachers
for the next thirty years, and none
will ever want to go into another line of work.
Whatever happens to the tenure system,
institutions could counterbalance the incentive
to permanence with a program of insurance
for mid-career changes. If a faculty member
decided, in mid-career, to leave academic life
for another vocation, the insurance plan
would provide basic support
during a few years of retraining
or of becoming established in a new field.**

---

To receive the benefits, a professor would of course have to resign his or her appointment and declare an intention to enter a non-academic field. The leaving of a tenured faculty member would allow his or her institution, in many cases, to hire a younger person instead, thus saving money, and in any case, to add new vigor to a faculty largely frozen into place by tenure and a tight job market. Insurance to make a mid-career change possible would create remarkable new opportunities both for professors and for institutions. Although many professors would never claim this insurance, they would benefit indirectly by having a lively new colleague in place of a person who, in many cases, had been doing the college no good.

Arguably, premiums for this insurance ought to come from individual professors, on the ground that any one of them might find that he or she will eventually want to take advantage of the benefits. If the program were voluntary, most young faculty members would probably feel they were unlikely ever to want to leave a field they were only then making such an effort to enter, and would therefore not sign up for the insurance.

Another possibility is that the institution could pay the premiums on behalf of each professor as a fringe benefit, hedging against the consequences of offering tenure. Only a fraction of faculty would ever seriously consider giving up a secure job even if insurance benefits could ease their way into a new kind of work. Nonetheless, that fraction could make a big difference to the climate of an institution, and possibly even save money. If the tenure system were modified or replaced by a system of increasingly longer contracts, for example, the need for mid-career transition insurance would remain, although the advantage would then fall mainly to the individual rather than to the institution. In any case, it is both humane and practical to provide support that opens a new career to a professor who can no longer do his or her best work in the academic world.

---

**Only a fraction of faculty would ever seriously consider giving up a secure job even if insurance benefits could ease their way into a new kind of work. Nonetheless, that fraction could make a big difference to the climate of an institution, and possibly even save money. It is both humane and practical to provide support that opens a new career to a professor who can no longer do his or her best work in the academic world.**

---

The chief disadvantage of the insurance plan would be that a prepaid transition period might offer a greater incentive to the adventurous and enterprising than to the dull and weary, causing an institution to lose some of its liveliest professors and having no effect on the very people who are contributing least to the institution. It is not likely, however, that professors who are highly valued would be tempted into leaving simply because they could claim transitional support. On the other hand, a person who saw quite clearly that he or she was no longer wanted by the institution could afford to leave only if the support were available.

In addition to mid-career transition insurance, colleges and universities could also do more to help professors who want to stay in academic life but who need stimulation and changes of pace beyond those described earlier. For example, a widespread program of faculty exchanges among institutions would allow professors to meet and work with new colleagues, use the facilities of other institutions, and broaden their experience of the academic world—all at virtually no cost to the institutions involved. Professors on exchange could continue to be paid by their own institutions so that the transactions would have no financial aspect. A couple of professors might tentatively agree upon a mutually satisfactory exchange, and then seek approval from their respective departments or other academic units. In a period when a high percentage of faculty were tenured, and when tight budgets did not permit new hiring except to replace professors as they retired, a vigorous and flexible program of faculty exchanges would offer a certain relief from a small-town atmosphere that might otherwise hang over many departments.

Finally, a new program is needed for professors who want opportunities for their own development less drastic than leaving academic life but more flexible than those that simply teaching at another institution through an exchange program. Traditionally, sabbatical programs have allowed professors to take some time off at

---

**What we need is a comprehensive plan
that will provide full security and rights
for part-time faculty, a flexible system
of time-off credits not tied
to any one college or university
or to any fixed cycle of years,
an insurance plan to facilitate mid-career
transitions out of the tenured ranks
and into a new academic field
or into nonacademic work, and programs
allowing faculty both to retire partially
before the usual age of 65 and to continue
working part time, in some cases, after that age.**

---

fixed intervals, provided that they stayed at a particular institution long enough to be eligible, and in some cases, provided that their proposal for spending the time was approved by whomever was in charge when the sabbatical came due. Unfortunately, the developmental needs of professors do not always coincide exactly with the cycle of the magic number seven, nor do they always require one long time off, rather than several shorter periods.

In place of the sabbatical system, colleges and universities could pay time-off credits into a national fund, again similar to TIAA-CREF. Credits would be paid not once every seven years, as now, but divided into monthly installments. Once paid into the fund, they would become the property of each faculty member, to be drawn upon whenever he or she could take leaves. The fund could arrange installments that would match what the existing sabbatical program costs each institution. A flexible program of credits that could be used at times when a professor most needed them could become much more popular than the present sabbatical system, and this provision for time-off might have implications far beyond the academic system. People in other fields might well set up time-off plans supported by funds paid as part of employee benefits and held on behalf of individuals, rather than tied to any employer.

Although retirement falls beyond the possibilities of making mid-career transitions, clearly the options of honorably shifting to part-time work before age 65 and of being invited to remain part-time after that age are in the same spirit of flexibility. So are plans to offer tenure to part-time faculty. All of these plans involve some exception to the normal course of full-time academic work, and plans made to serve one need will inevitably affect others. What we need is a comprehensive plan that will provide full security and rights for part-time faculty, a flexible system of time-off credits not tied to any one college or university or to any fixed cycle of years, an insurance plan to facilitate mid-career transitions out of the tenured ranks and into a new academic field or into nonacademic work, and programs allowing faculty both to retire partially before the usual age of 65 and to continue working part-time, in some cases, after that age.

---

Ed. note: The idea of a national faculty career insurance program deserves serious study by institutions of higher learning, insurance organizations, and foundations alike. Although its practical application would be complex, the underlying principles are relatively simple. It begins with an assumption that both incremental inflation and a zero-growth rate in the higher education system make declining academic employment over the next two decades inevitable. The natural turnover of the American faculty pool has also slowed considerably, due to the current high ratio of tenured faculty and the relatively small percentage of retirement-age academics. Some further breathing space for new blood should also be provided at the lowest ranks, so as to assure continued entrypoints to the most talented doctoral students and instructors during this period of retrenchment.

It is not likely that such an insurance pool would work on anything but a mandatory basis. Assuming, for the sake of illustration, an insurable pool of 300,000 academics, and a gross mid-career drop-off rate of 3 percent annually beyond those of normal retirement age, 9,000 ex-academics could claim such benefits each year. If benefits were pegged at 100 percent of final salary for the first year and 50 percent for a second (but terminated at the time of successful reemployment within these two years), some estimates of the necessary money pool can be made. If average salaries are estimated at $18,000 annually at the assistant and associate professorial rank, with $9,000 provided for a second year, assuming no successful reemployment, the funding provision necessary for the average claimant would total $27,000. Thus, the total insurance pool necessary each year would be $24,300,000 ($27,000 times 9,000 drop-offs). If spread equally among 300,000 policyholders, the annual premium would be $810 above present insurance contributions. In order to get such a mechanism going, some massive initial funding would become necessary. Obviously, year-by-year experience would determine the viability of these assumptions, but this will illustrate one of many possible approaches to helping ease professional academics into other walks of life. Needless to say, the requirements for control, means tests, and eligibility determinations pose serious additional challenges.

# 12

## Ways
## to
## Begin

Seven key recommendations, and a discussion of how they would work. Strategies on how to begin revitalizing campus teaching, their hazards and their pay-offs. If the sixties was the decade of growth, the seventies and eighties can well become the decades of resourcefulness.

UPON HEARING A DETAILED PROPOSAL FOR HIS OWN IM-
provement, a man is said to have replied: "The plan will never work;
it's already been done, and besides I thought of it first." After initial
resistance and distrust, we hope to elicit the serious questions that
any program of faculty development must address as it begins. We
want briefly to summarize seven key recommendations and then to
propose ways of finding the resources necessary for a new program
and ways of organizing it. Here, then, are the key recommendations:

1. Colleges and universities should organize regular campus programs on teaching, coordinated by an institute, supported out of the
general budget, and sustained primarily by faculty themselves, using
roughly 10 percent of their professional time for activities they now
neglect. The purpose of the institute should be to create and sustain
a pedagogical culture on campus, primarily through directly observing and discussing many examples of teaching, rather than through
theoretical lectures on pedagogy or second-hand accounts of teaching. Whatever use is made of consultants or a professional staff, the
responsibility for making the program work should rest with members of the faculty—some of whom, as associates, would devote part
of their regular teaching time to the work of the institute.

2. Universities bear a responsibility both for their own teaching of
undergraduates and for the later teaching of those whom they
award higher degrees. Therefore, the campus institute should
supervise a teaching practicum undertaken by graduate students in
the course of their work for the PhD or other degrees that lead to
work in college teaching. These students would learn not only by
doing but by disciplined self-reflection, supervision, observation of
other teachers, and detailed discussion.

3. Graduate students should be able to have their teaching officially evaluated for the record by methods that aim to be as sophisticated as those used to judge their scholarship. Teaching should be
judged by a variety of observers who would produce not a "grade"
but a statement of mastery, describing what the student has shown

he or she can do. The university would support this system just as it certifies competence in scholarship.

Entirely separate from these official evaluations, the teaching institute should provide confidential assessments of work done by graduate students and professors alike. These would not be recorded and would be a matter strictly between the observers and the teacher. This kind of assessment would involve much more of the institute's time and attention than would the official evaluations made for the record.

4. Just as college teachers should have access to separate systems of confidential assessment and official certification of their teaching, so college students should be graded for the record by people other than their own teachers. A system of certification by third parties can free the teaching relationship from the often unacknowledged conflict between the roles of teacher as helper and teacher as judge. If teachers, like other professionals such as physicians and attorneys, could sustain a confidential relationship with students and leave the judging to others, students would be less inhibited about revealing what they do not know, less driven to feign understanding. Under this system, professors would not be free from having to certify mastery, but they could examine students other than their own.

5. Professors should have access to small grants for special teaching projects. At present, only research proposals are likely to bring in money. But if even a small percentage of the total educational budget were set aside for this purpose—especially if the grants were linked with the campus teaching institute—the inventiveness of professors might emerge more fully in the sphere of teaching.

6. Institutions should loosen the present monopoly departments now hold over both professorial time and the "fields" of knowledge. Alongside the departmental structure, institutions could encourage the development of colleague groups devoted, like departments, to teaching as well as research. In this system, a given professor would have a multiple identity, as both a political scientist, let us say, and a member of a colleague group on the allocation of world resources. A collateral system of colleague groups will work only to the extent that it shares the powers of departments.

7. In mid-career some professors develop nonacademic ambitions, want to switch to another field within academic life, or become disinterested in teaching. In order to allow them seriously to consider changing careers, we need a system of insurance for mid-career changes that is open to all colleges and universities. Under this system, a professor who left a senior position and declared an intention of taking up another field would receive funds to facilitate the transition. This would provide a way out for the individual professor and would make funds available to the institution for a fresh appointment.

Many of these recommendations are directed at the state of pedagogical solitude in which most college teachers learn and practice their art. As department members, researchers, and committee members, faculty enjoy various forms of colleagueship, but as teachers they generally work alone. A program for faculty development begins with the recognition that the quality of teaching depends not only on scholarship but on pedagogical colleagueship.

To be sure, individual professors could make certain improve-

ments on their own by reading about education and student development, by experimenting in their own courses, and by observing the
results systematically. Institutions could encourage some improvement simply by starting to give greater weight to student evaluations
of teaching in decisions that affect professors' careers. However,
colleges and universities should develop separate systems for mutu-
al observation of classes by colleagues and other suitable people.
Visitors can come from the teacher's own department, other departments at the same institution, and from departments in the same
field at neighboring institutions.

Once an institution accepts the value of alternatives to pedagogical solitude, it faces the question of how to support a program of
faculty development. In the years of easy expansion, colleges and
universities came to assume that starting a new program would generally require a grant. In the case of faculty development, however,
the main requirement is not cash but a fraction of the professors'
time.

Reformers have often assumed an automatic resistance on the
part of faculty and academic departments to serious programs to
improve teaching. However, part of this resistance has sprung not
from an unwillingness to make the necessary effort but from a lack
of knowledge about how to improve and a sense that such knowledge was not really available. A recent survey found that, even at a
major research university, nearly half of the faculty was willing to
engage in a formal training program to improve the quality of their
work with students. Presumably the percentage is even higher at
colleges that impose less severe demands for publication.

No program will thrive unless faculty find a place for it within
their normal working hours. Therefore, a program of faculty development should begin by helping professors analyze how they use
their time so they can reallocate about ten percent of it to work in
the program. This might amount to four, five, perhaps six hours a
week. Teachers know how much time they spend in class, but few
can accurately say how much they spend, in a typical week, on preparing for class, dealing with papers and exams, meeting with individual students or committees, talking with colleagues, responding
to questionnaires or requests for recommendations, doing various
kinds of research or writing, and so forth. Occasionally, legislatures
or administrators have required faculty to account for their time,
and this can always plausibly be done—especially if the only purpose is to document the claim that professors spend a lot of time on
the job and a reasonable fraction of it with, or on behalf of, students. What faculty should do now, however, is to analyze their use
of time for their own benefit, making fresh judgments about what is
most valuable.

Assuming that faculty can find the necessary time, how can the
program come into being? It would not be unusual in the academic
world for a committee to study all aspects of the proposal for a year
or more and then put the question to the faculty for a vote. Even if
the proposal were finally approved, its opponents might have fatally
weakened it. If the program involved all faculty, it might then be
sabotaged through passive resistance and self-defensive carping
from within. If it were only for volunteers, it might nonetheless lose
many potential volunteers by having become "controversial."

Fortunately, there are other ways to proceed. Organizers of a faculty development program might start with a small, well-sponsored, and carefully organized program designed for those professors who most want to take advantage of it. If the program required no more than a modest financial outlay, and if it were imposed on no one, its organizers should face a minimum of delaying tactics, raucous debate or demands for formal authorization. This would have several advantages. It would reduce polarization on the issues raised. It would make services immediately available. It would allow participants to help one another without being diverted by those untouched by the spirit of the enterprise. And the program could spread by the force of example.

---

Reformers have often assumed an automatic resistance
on the part of faculty and academic departments to
serious programs to improve teaching. However,
part of this resistance has sprung not
from an unwillingness to make the necessary effort
but from a lack of knowledge about
how to improve and a sense that such knowledge
was not really available. A recent
survey found that, even at a major
research university, nearly half of the faculty
was willing to engage in a formal training
program to improve the quality of their
work with students. Presumably
the percentage is even higher at colleges
that impose less severe demands for publication.

---

One danger of starting only with volunteer faculty is that they might include a high percentage of professors most disaffected from the institution. The program could thus become known as a haven for "misfits." Another danger is that if certain professors were encouraged to take part, a rumor might start to the effect that the program existed to offer compensatory education to "incompetents." The organizers should therefore make a deliberate and concerted effort to recruit people highly respected in the institution as well as some of the best teachers on campus. Such professors should participate in the day-to-day affairs of the program, as well as serving as sponsors and advisers. The program should always include various degrees of competence, status, and conventionality.

Such a program need not be defined as "experimental," any more than it need become a "requirement." It can be open to everyone. As people come to appreciate its value, participating in it can be officially recognized as satisfying a fraction of a professor's pedagogical duties. Personnel committees can take account of contributions made to the program and evidence of teaching effectiveness shown within it.

The next decade will not be easy for professors. Economic and social pressures will require a new level of resourcefulness. Faculty will seek to protect their economic interests in a variety of ways, including group action; but ultimately their well-being depends on support for higher education by taxpayers, potential students, and donors. Whatever self-defensive measures are required, faculty should place their main hope in programs for professional development. To the extent that faculty development thrives, colleges and universities will have more to offer the public and professors will at the same time find greater satisfaction in their work.

# Further Reading

The scholarly literature on higher education is extensive. This brief list focuses mainly on human development in colleges and universities, especially that of faculty members, on the training of teachers, the social setting of academic work, and the practice and evaluation of teaching. These selections are intended to suggest the range and development of knowledge in these areas. Many of the items cited contain bibliographies.

Professors with a special interest in teaching have been able to turn to such books as Gilbert Highet's *The Art of Teaching* (Knopf, 1950), an urbane essay organized around "suggestions drawn from practice"; Wilbert J. McKeachie's *Teaching Tips* (D.C. Heath and Co., 1951, now in its sixth edition), a step-by-step guidebook based largely on research by psychologists; *The Importance of Teaching: A Memorandum to the New College Teacher*, the report of the Committee on Undergraduate Teaching (Hazen Foundation, 1968); and *Effective College Teaching*, edited by William H. Morris (American Council on Education, 1970), a collection of essays on teaching in a variety of fields.

Some books useful for general background on the role of faculty are *The American College*, edited by Nevitt Sanford (Wiley, 1962), the pioneering, 1,084-page "psychological and social interpretation of the higher learning," much of it still fresh today; Laurence R. Veysey's *The Emergence of the American University* (University of Chicago Press, 1965), an historical study of the years 1865 to 1910 which clarifies many of the constraints on the faculty role; and *The Academic Revolution* by Christopher Jencks and David Riesman (Doubleday, 1968), an account of the rise of professional scholars and scientists, a theory about the development of higher education, and a critique of some of its present faults.

A variety of approaches to faculty development are reflected in *Improving College Teaching*, edited by Calvin B.T. Lee (American Council on Education, 1967); Florence B. Brawer's *Personality Characteristics of College and University Faculty* (ERIC Clearinghouse for Junior College Information/American Association of Junior Colleges, 1968); Kiyo Morimoto's "Supervising Teachers in Groups," in *Supervision: The Reluctant Profession*, edited by Ralph Moser and David Purpel (Houghton-Mifflin, 1972); *The Teaching Environment: A Study of Optimum Working Conditions for Effective College Teaching*, by Jerry G. Gaff and Robert C. Wilson (Center for Research and Development in Higher Education, 1971), and by the same authors, "Faculty Values and Improving Teaching," in *New Teaching, New Learning*, edited by G. Kerry Smith (Jossey-Bass, 1971); Nevitt Sanford's "Academic Culture and the Teacher's Development," *Soundings*, Winter 1971; Kenneth Eble's *Professors as Teachers* (Jossey-Bass, 1972); "The Ills of College Teaching: Diagnosis and Prescription," by Raymond P. Whitefield and Lawrence M. Brammer, in *Journal of Higher Education*, January 1973; and *Facilitating Faculty Development*, edited by Mervin Freedman, issue number 1, *New Directions for Higher Education* (Jossey-Bass, Spring 1973).

The literature on student development includes such writings as Nevitt Sanford's "The Developmental Status of the Entering Freshman," in *The American College* (cited above); Esther Rauschenbush's *The Student and His Studies* (Wesleyan University Press, 1964); *The Student in Higher Education*, a report sponsored and published by the Hazen Foundation (1968); *No Time for Youth*, edited by Joseph Katz (Jossey-Bass, 1968), especially the first and last chapters; Arthur W. Chickering's *Education and Identity* (Jossey-Bass, 1969); *The Impact of College on Students*, by Kenneth A. Feldman and Theodore M. Newcomb (Jossey-Bass, 1969); *Forms of Intellectual and Ethical Development in the College Years*, by William G. Perry, Jr. (Holt, Rinehart and Winston, 1970); Benson R. Synder's *The Hidden Curriculum* (Knopf, 1971); and *Lighting a Fire in the University: A Primer for Reform*, by Craig Eisendrath and Thomas Cottle (Schenkman, 1972).

Close observation of what actually occurs in classrooms is rare, but examples can be found in chapters 9 and 10 of *The American College* (cited above); Martin Duberman's "An Experiment in Education," *Daedalus*, Winter 1968; *The College Classroom: Conflict, Change, and Learning*, by Richard D. Mann and others (Wiley, 1970); several articles in *Change* Magazine, including "Teaching: The Uncertain Profession," a discussion published in April 1972, Brent Harold's "Beyond Student-Centered Teaching," October 1972, and Elaine G. Breslaw's "Behaviorism in the Classroom," April 1973; and Joseph Axelrod's *The University Teacher as Artist* (Jossey-Bass, 1973).

For discussions of the training needed by future professors and of what they receive in graduate schools, see such studies as Paul Klapper's "The Professional Preparation of the College Teacher," *Journal of General Education*, 1949; *The Preparation of College Teachers*, edited by T.C. Blegen and R.M. Cooper (American Council on Education, 1950); J.S. Diekhoff's *Tomorrow's Professors: A Report of the College Faculty Internship Program* (Fund for the Advancement of Education, 1960); J.P. Miller's "A Report on Graduate Education at Yale," *Ventures*, Fall 1966, and "Reorganization of the Teaching Assistantship: An Interim Report," *Ventures*, Spring 1967; *The Graduate Student as Teacher* by Vincent Nowlis, Kenneth E. Clark, and Miriam Rock (American Council on Education, 1968); *Challenges to Graduate Schools* by Ann Heiss (Jossey-Bass, 1970); and Richard J. Storr's *The Beginning of the Future: A Historical Approach to Graduate Education in the Arts and Sciences* (McGraw-Hill, 1973).

The evaluation of pedagogical methods is discussed by W.J. McKeachie in chapter 8 of *The American College* (cited above) and in "Research on Teaching at the College and University Level," in *Handbook of Research on Teaching*, edited by N.L. Gage (Rand McNally, 1963); and the evaluation of teachers by several authors in part 5 of the volume edited by Lee (cited above), including "Current Practices in the Evaluation and Training of College Teachers," by Alexander W. Astin and Calvin B.T. Lee; and also by Richard I. Miller in *Developing Programs for Faculty Evaluation* (Jossey-Bass, 1974), which has a very long annotated bibliography. The effects of grading on students are examined in *Making the Grade* by Howard S. Becker, Blanche Geer, and Everett C. Hughes (Wiley, 1968), and in *The Hidden Curriculum* (cited above).

The sociology of faculty life is discussed in such writings as Burton R. Clark's "Faculty Organization and Authority," in *Professionalization*, edited by H.M. Vollmer and D.L. Mills (Prentice-Hall, 1966); Jill Conway's "Styles of Academic Culture," *Daedalus*, Winter 1970; *The Impact of the Academic Revolution on Faculty Careers*, by D.W. Light, Jr., L.R. Marsden, and T.C. Corl (American Association for Higher Education, 1972); the Winter 1974 issue of *Sociology of Education*, devoted entirely to new research on the sociology of faculty and edited by D.W. Light, Jr.; and in such publications by David Riesman as "The Academic Career: Notes on Recruitment and Colleagueship," *Daedalus*, Winter 1959; "Notes on Meritocracy," *Daedalus*, Summer 1967; *Academic Values and Mass Education*, written with Joseph Gusfield and Zelda Gamson (Doubleday, 1970); and "Notes on Educational Reform," *Journal of General Education*, July 1971.

# A Documentary on Innovations in Undergraduate Education

A new 52-minute color documentary on some of higher education's most significant new curricular innovations is now available to concerned faculty. Highly lauded by the editors of Change, this significant documentary was produced in 1974 by the Center for Improvement of Undergraduate Education at Cornell University. For further information on showings to faculty and administrators, contact the Center at Department M, Rand Hall, Cornell University, Ithaca, N.Y. 14850

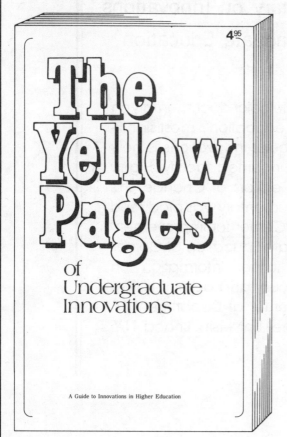

For additional copies of

FACULTY DEVELOPMENT
IN A TIME OF RETRENCHMENT

address your order to:

**CHANGE Book Department**
**NBW Tower**
**New Rochelle, N.Y. 10801**


$2.95 per copy if payment accompanies order
$3.95 per copy if billing preferred
$1.95 per copy for orders of 10 books or more ($19.50 minimum
   order; use office letterhead if billing is preferred)


**Please be sure to include your name,**
**address and zip code with your order.**